Viva Studymates

Perfect Grammar

How to Recognise, Correct and Avoid Grammatical Errors

Viva Studymates

Perfect Grammar

How to Recognise, Correct and Avoid Grammatical Errors

Dr Derek Soles

Viva Books

New Delhi | Mumbai | Chennai | Kolkata | Bangalore | Hyderabad | Kochi | Guwahati

First Indian Edition 2010
Reprinted 2012

VIVA BOOKS PRIVATE LIMITED

- 4737/23 Ansari Road, Daryaganj, New Delhi 110 002
  E-mail: vivadelhi@vivagroupindia.net, Tel. 42242200
- Plot No. 76, Service Industries, Shirvane, Sector 1, Nerul, Navi Mumbai 400 706
  E-mail: vivamumbai@vivagroupindia.net, Tel. 27721273, 27721274
- Jamals Fazal Chambers, 26 Greams Road, Chennai 600 006
  E-mail: vivachennai@vivagroupindia.net, Tel. 28290304, 28294241
- B-103, Jindal Towers, 21/1A/3 Darga Road, Kolkata 700 017
  E-mail: vivakolkata@vivagroupindia.net, Tel. 22836381, 22816713
- 7, Sovereign Park Apartments, 56-58, K. R. Road, Basavanagudi, Bangalore 560 004
  E-mail: vivabangalore@vivagroupindia.net, Tel. 26607409, 26607410
- 101-102 Mughal Marc Apartments, 3-4-637 to 641, Narayanguda, Hyderabad 500 029
  E-mail: vivahyderabad@vivagroupindia.net, Tel. 27564481, 27564482
- Beevi Towers, First Floor, SRM Road, Kaloor, Kochi 682 018, Kerala
  E-mail: vivakochi@vivagroupindia.net, Tel: 0484-2403055, 2403056
- 232, GNB Road, Beside UCO Bank, Silpukhuri, Guwahati 781 003
  E-mail: vivaguwahati@vivagroupindia.net, Tel: 0361-2666386

www.vivagroupindia.com

Published by arrangement with
Studymates Limited
PO Box 2, Bishops Lydeard,
Somerset TA4 3YE,
United Kingdom

ISBN : 978-81-309-1306-3

Published by Vinod Vasishtha for Viva Books Private Limited, 4737/23, Ansari Road, New Delhi-110 002. Printed and bound by Raj Press, R-3, Inderpuri, New Delhi - 110 012.

L0000 / L0100

To Nin

Contents

Preface

I have been an English professor for many years, and I have regularly experienced the occupational hazard of my profession: phone calls and emails from students, former students, friends, and sometimes complete strangers, seeking an answer to a question about proper English grammar. Here are three recent enquires:

1. Do I write 'neither of the bills for your services was sent or were sent to the proper address?'
2. Which is correct: 'I hope you can give my wife and I a ride or I hope you can give my wife and me a ride?'
3. Help! I say this sentence is correct as is: 'The headmaster, whom I believe has been at the school for less than a year, has no right to change the policy without informing parents'. Marion insists 'whom' should be 'who'. Who is right? We have bet dinner at the White Dog.

These students and friends have convinced me that there is a need for a clear and concise, yet thorough, guide to the grammar of an English sentence. The purpose of *Perfect Grammar* is to meet this need. This book will help you write those letters, emails, essays, and reports with greater confidence by guiding you through the rules of English grammar. You will learn from this book the conventions of Standard English, especially those that are often violated.

You will learn, for example, why 'was sent' is the correct verb for question 1 above. The sentence's subject is 'neither', a singular subject, which requires a singular verb—'was sent', not the plural verb 'were sent'. (See Chapter Seven.) You will learn why 'me' is the correct pronoun for sentence two. A verb—in this sentence, the verb 'give'—must be followed by an objective not a subjective case pronoun: Give me a ride, not Give I a ride. (See Chapter Six.) And you will learn why Marion's husband owes her dinner. The verb 'has been' requires a subject; 'who' never 'whom' provides a subject for a verb. (See Chapter Six.)

Perfect Grammar begins with a Chapter that explains the anatomy of an English sentence. This is an important Chapter in that it will provide definitions of the key terms you will need to know to understand the grammar errors explained in subsequent Chapters, and it will, therefore, make it easier for you to avoid these errors in your own writing. Chapters Two through Nine discuss common grammar errors, specifying when, why, how, and where writers make these errors. These chapters explain how to spot errors when you are revising your writing, and they offer ways of correcting the errors to make your sentences perfect.

Chapter Two teaches you how to avoid the sentence fragment, that stream of phrases and clauses that begins with a capital letter and ends with a period but does not manage to form a complete sentence. It explains, as well, those circumstances under which the sentence fragment is an acceptable, even effective, rhetorical stratagem.

Chapter Three explains the causes of the run-on sentence, that sequence of clauses that is punctuated as one sentence but needs to be either revised or divided into two separate sentences.

Chapter Four describes the many enemies of sentence clarity—faulty parallelism, misplaced and dangling modifiers, shifts in voice and point-of-view, wordiness, faulty predication—and offers strategies for avoiding ambiguity and for writing clear sentences.

Chapter Five discusses pronoun reference and agreement. It offers advice on how to make readers know which noun it is that a writer's pronoun is referencing. And it discusses pronoun agreement, a controversial topic at a time when writers must be sensitive to the fact that an astronaut or a surgeon or a midfielder can be a he or a she, a him or a her.

Chapter Six continues our discussion of pronouns, focusing on pronoun case. This chapter explains the differences in pronoun case and when to use the subjective, objective, and possessive case of the pronoun.

Chapter Seven explains subject-verb agreement. It explains which verb to use when you have more than one subject; which verb to use when your subject is an indefinite pronoun such as none or all or each or neither; and which verb to use when your subject is a collective noun such as press, team, orchestra, or crew.

Chapter Eight discusses verb tense. How do you know if you need to use different tenses in the same sentence? What is the difference between a verb in the past tense (waited, for example) and its present perfect tense form (has waited)? What is the difference between present tense (she waits) and progressive tense (she is waiting)? This Chapter answers these and other related questions.

Chapter Nine turns our attention to the rules of punctuation, insofar as these rules relate to and depend upon proper English grammar.

Chapter Ten turns our attention to the relationship between grammar and usage, explaining a dozen common errors in usage and how to avoid them.

In accordance with the Studymates mission, *Perfect Grammar* explains clearly and concisely, yet thoroughly, how to improve your writing by recognising, avoiding, and correcting grammar errors.

1 The anatomy of an English sentence

One-minute overview

The aim of the Chapter is to introduce you to the terminology you will need in order to understand completely the subsequent chapters, which will detail common errors in grammar and explain how you can avoid them. Key terms, including noun, subject, verb, predicate, object, preposition, prepositional phrase, adjective, adverb, and clause, will be defined and explained in this Chapter in the context of complete sentences. The sentences will increase in complexity—from simple to compound to complex to compound-complex—as the Chapter proceeds.

The simple sentence

A simple sentence contains a single subject and a single verb. A subject is a noun or a pronoun responsible for performing the action which the verb specifies. A noun is a word that identifies a person, a place, or a thing, including a state of mind such as happiness or revulsion; a pronoun is a small word that takes the place of a noun so the noun does not have to be repeated, so we can write 'David met his father', instead of 'David met David's father'. A verb is a word that usually identifies an action, though the very common verb 'to be' identifies more a state of existence than an action. Here is an example of a simple sentence:

Belfast is prospering.

The noun-subject of the sentence is 'Belfast' and the verb-predicate is 'is prospering'.

A simple sentence might also contain a word that receives the action of the verb. Here is an example:

Belfast hosted the conference.

In this sentence, 'Belfast' is the subject, 'hosted' is the verb, and 'conference' is the word that receives the action of the verb, indicating what Belfast hosted. This word, usually a noun or pronoun, is called the object of the verb, more specifically the direct object of the verb.

A simple sentence might also contain a noun or pronoun that widens the context of the direct object. Consider this sentence.

The Lord Mayor of Belfast gave Dr. Whitman the award.

The subject is 'Lord Mayor', the verb is 'gave', and the direct object is 'award'. Remember the direct object is the receiver of the action of the verb: the mayor did not give Dr. Whitman; the mayor gave the award. He gave the award to Dr. Whitman. We call such a word, usually a noun or a pronoun, which widens the context of the direct object, the indirect object of the sentence.

Now consider this simple sentence:

Belfast is a beautiful city.

This sentence seems to follow the subject-verb-object pattern of 'Belfast hosted the conference'. But notice this important difference: 'Belfast' and 'conference' identify different entities, but 'Belfast' and 'city' identify the same entity. The verb 'is' links together two things that are the same. The verb 'is' is a form of the verb 'to be'. It is called a copula verb, as distinct from the action verb 'hosted'. 'Belfast' is still the subject of the sentence but 'city' is not the object of the verb because it is not receiving the action of the verb. It complements the subject and, thus, is called a subject complement.

We have, then, four simple sentence patterns:

1. Subject-verb
2. Subject-verb-direct object

3. Subject-verb-indirect object-direct object
4. Subject-copula verb-subject complement.

Now a simple sentence can be and usually is fleshed out with other words and phrases. The noun-subjects and noun-objects might be qualified or clarified with other words, known as adjectives: Belfast is a <u>beautiful</u> city. It hosted an <u>excellent</u> conference. The verbs might be qualified or clarified with other words, known as adverbs: The neighbourhoods in Belfast are still <u>highly</u> segregated. Adverbs can also qualify adjectives—Belfast is a <u>very</u> beautiful city.

A simple sentence can also be fleshed out with phrases. A phrase is a group of words which does not contain the subject-verb sentence pattern but which modifies nouns and verbs in a sentence. The most common type of phrase is the prepositional phrase, which begins with a preposition and ends with a noun or pronoun, called the object of the preposition, as opposed to the object of the verb. A preposition is a short word that establishes links among verbs, nouns, and pronouns within a sentence. Common prepositions include these words: by, for, to, in, with, near, from, out, into, about. Study this sentence carefully:

> With its new sports centre, fine restaurants, and designer shops, Belfast is becoming a popular destination for low-cost airlines from Britain and Europe, for shoppers from the Irish Republic, and for business conferences.

Although long, this is a simple sentence consisting of a subject, a copula verb, and a complement—Belfast is becoming a destination—and a series of prepositional phrases. Each of these phrases begins with a preposition and ends with a noun—the object of the preposition. They are:

With its new sports centre, fine restaurants, and designer shops (modifies 'Belfast');
for low-cost airlines (modifies 'destination');
from Britain and Europe (modifies 'airlines');
for shoppers (modifies 'destination');
from the Irish Republic (modifies 'shoppers');
for business conferences (modifies 'destination').

A digression: Ending a sentence with a preposition

It is common to hear a preposition at the end of a sentence in casual speech and informal writing: I don't know what this poem is about. It was my first day of work, and I did not even know who I was supposed to report to. It's not his mind she is interested in. A preposition is not a word you should end a sentence with.

In formal speech and writing, though, it is best to avoid a preposition at the end of a sentence: I don't understand this poem. It was my first day of work, and I did not even know to whom I was supposed to report. It's not his mind in which she is interested. A preposition is not a word with which you should end a sentence.

The compound sentence

A compound sentence consists of two simple sentences, joined together by a comma plus a coordinate conjunction, a semi-colon, or a colon. A coordinate conjunction is a small word—'and', 'but', and 'or' are the most common—that links together words, phrases, or clauses. Suppose, for example, we wanted to link together these two simple sentences: A new James Bond movie has just been released. Critics are hailing it as the best Bond film in years. We could use the comma plus the coordinate conjunction:

> A new James Bond movie has just been released, and critics are hailing it as the best Bond film in years.

We could also use a coordinate conjunction to link together these two sentences: A new James Bond movie has just been released. Critics complain it is not as good as the earlier ones:

> A new James Bond movie has just been released, but critics complain it is not as good as the earlier ones.

Note that the comma is there only if it and the coordinate conjunction are linking together complete sentences. You would use a comma and a coordinate conjunction in this sentence:

A new James Bond movie has just been released, and it will debut in Birmingham on Friday.

But if you chose to delete the pronoun 'it', the subject of the second sentence, you would no longer have a compound sentence, but a simple sentence with two verbs, 'has just been released' and 'will debut'. If you chose to write the sentence this way, you would delete the comma, as well.

A new James Bond movie has just been released and will debut in Birmingham on Friday.

Writers can also join simple sentences together to form a compound sentence with a semi-colon, as long as the two sentences deal with the same topic.

A new James Bond movie has just been released; it is getting rave reviews.

Finally, you can join together two simple sentences with a colon, but only if the second sentence elaborates on some aspect of the first sentence:

Reviews of the new Bond movie are not good: critics are saying it is poorly cast and not engaging.

The complex sentence

A complex sentence consists of a simple sentence, plus a dependent clause. A clause is a group of words that contains a subject and a verb. Some clauses, therefore, specifically independent or main clauses, are exactly the same as a sentence. But other clauses, called dependent or subordinate clauses, are less than a sentence. Consider this simple sentence:

Airbus is Europe's largest commercial aircraft manufacturer.

This is a simple sentence, a main clause, an independent clause. But watch what happens when we add a word to the beginning of the sentence:

> Although Airbus is Europe's largest commercial aircraft manufacturer…

Now we have changed this into a dependent or subordinate clause because it can no longer stand alone as a sentence. The word 'although' (called a subordinate conjunction) reduces what was a complete sentence because it implies more must be said to make a meaningful statement. We need to add a simple sentence (a main or independent clause) to this subordinate (or dependent) clause to complete its meaning. In so doing, we create a complex sentence.

> Although Airbus is Europe's largest commercial aircraft manufacturer, its executives earn less than executives who work for smaller companies.

Note that this distinction between independent (main) and dependent (subordinate) clauses will become very important when we discuss sentence fragments in the next Chapter.

Our sentence could be expressed, of course, as a compound sentence:

> Airbus is Europe's largest commercial aircraft manufacturer, but its executives earn less than executives who work for smaller companies.

And there are other ways to express it as a complex sentence. The subordinate (dependent) clauses are underlined.

> Airbus, <u>which is Europe's largest commercial aircraft manufacturer</u>, pays its executives less than smaller companies pay theirs.

> Airbus did not attract the best-qualified applicants, <u>because it pays its executives less than smaller companies pay theirs</u>.

Note that in the first sentence above, the dependent (subordinate) clause is functioning as an adjective, in that it is describing or modifying the noun 'Airbus'. In the second sentence, the subordinate clause is acting as an adverb, in that it is explaining why Airbus did not attract, the verb in the sentence, the best qualified applicants.

In addition to acting as an adjective or as an adverb, a clause can act as a noun. A noun is usually a subject or an object in a sentence, and so, too, is a noun clause. Consider these sentences:

1. Whoever has the most experience will have an advantage.
2. What we need now are good applicants.
3. I know who is going to get the job.
4. I know that Airbus is a good company.
5. The executive committee will give the job to whoever has the most experience.

The first two sentences above have noun clauses acting as subjects. The verb in the first sentence is 'will have'. The subject is not simply 'Whoever', because the meaning of the sentence is not 'Whoever will have an advantage'. It is more restricted than this. It is 'Whoever has the most experience'. The entire clause, in other words, function as the subject. The same is true of the second sentence. The verb is 'are'. The subject is the noun clause 'What we need now'.

Sentences 3, 4, and 5 have noun clauses acting as objects. In the third sentence, the subject is 'I' and the verb is 'know'. Remember that a direct object will answer the question who or what after the verb. Hence, I know what? I know who is going to get the job. The noun clause is the sentence's direct object. The same is true for sentence 4. I know what? I know that Airbus is a good company. Remember, as well, that prepositions have objects. In Sentence 5, the preposition 'to' is followed by a noun clause, which functions as the object of the preposition. The executive committee will give the job to him. The executive committee will give the job to whoever has the most experience. Note that the correct pronoun is 'whoever' not 'whomever', for reasons that will be explained in Chapter Five.

The compound complex sentence

The compound-complex sentence consists of a compound sentence plus one or more dependent (or subordinate) clauses. Consider this sentence.

> While he was speaking in a town in the northwest of Iran, near the border with northern Iraq, Mr. Ahmadinejad told a crowd that the enemies of Iran were trying to stop the country pursuing its peaceful nuclear programme, but he promised that they would soon fail.

This sentence is compound-complex, because it contains two independent clauses:

> Mr. Ahmadinejad told a crowd.
> He promised.

And it contains three subordinate (dependent) clauses:

> While he was speaking...
> that the enemies of Iran were trying to stop the country;
> that they would soon fail.

Here is another example. The first clause in this sentence is subordinate and the other two are main:

> When Mr. Ahmadinejad spoke in Baneh, he told a large crowd that the enemies of Iran were trying to top the country pursuing its peaceful nuclear programme, but he promised the crowd these enemies would fail.

Here are two more examples of compound-complex sentences:

> Russia and China are Iran's major trading partners, and their governments are reluctant to condemn Ahmadinejad, even though the governments of Britain and the U.S. believe Iran is trying to develop nuclear weapons.

> The International Atomic Energy Agency is responsible for monitoring Iran's nuclear activities, but agency

officials have expressed frustration, because they cannot get access to the nuclear power plants.

Each of these sentences begins with a main clause, which ends with the comma, followed by another main clause, which ends with the comma, followed by the subordinate clause, which ends with the sentence's full stop.

Tutorial

Progress questions

In the following sentences, underline the subjects and highlight the verbs.

1. The economy of Afghanistan depends upon the opium trade.
2. Drug barons have considerable social and political power.
3. Efforts by British and American diplomats to stop the drug trade have not been successful.
4. In Afghanistan senior civil servants and prominent politicians profit from the sale of opium.
5. Afghan farmers pay local police officials to protect their crops.

In the following sentences, underline the objects of verbs and highlight the objects of prepositions.

1. With money from their opium harvest, Afghan farmers bribe local police officials.
2. Organised crime controls the distribution of opium around the world.
3. Political leaders distance themselves in public from drug traffickers.
4. A report from the UN Office on Drugs and Crime implicates officials in the Ministry of the Interior.
5. Farmers in some parts of the country could grow other profitable crops.

Define and provide an example of the following terms:

1. adjective
2. adverb
3. subject complement
4. copula verb
5. indirect object.

Compose a sentence based upon each of the following criteria.

1. A simple sentence about Easter.
2. A compound sentence about Wales.

3. A complex sentence about cricket.
4. A complex sentence about Stonehenge.
5. A compound-complex sentence about breakfast.

Discussion points

What is the difference between a dependent and an independent clause? Why is it important to know this?

Practical assignment

Write a paragraph that describes your career or a career you hope to have some day. Try, in your paragraph, to include at least one of each of the four sentence types: simple, compound, complex, compound-complex.

Study and revision tip

Remember that if you learn the anatomy of an English sentence, you will be less likely to commit grammar errors.

Answers to the progress questions

In the following sentences, underline the subjects and highlight the verbs.

1. The economy of Afghanistan depends upon the opium trade.
2. Drug barons have considerable social and political power.
3. Efforts by British and American diplomats to stop the drug trade have not been successful.
4. In Afghanistan senior civil servants and prominent politicians profit from the sale of opium.
5. Afghan farmers pay local police officials to protect their crops.

In the following sentences, underline the objects of verbs and highlight the objects of prepositions.

1. With money from their opium harvest, Afghan farmers bribe local police officials.
2. Organised crime controls the distribution of opium around the world.
3. Political leaders distance themselves in public from drug traffickers.

4. A report from the UN Office on Drugs and Crime implicates officials in the Ministry of the Interior.
5. Farmers in some parts of the country could grow other profitable crops.

Define and provide an example of the following terms.

1. adjective: a word that qualifies a noun or pronoun; examples will vary.
2. adverb: a word that qualifies a verb, an adjective, or another adverb; examples will vary.
3. subject complement: a word following a copula verb which identifies or qualifies the subject of the copula verb; examples will vary.
4. copula verb: a verb that links together a subject and a complement; the verb 'to be' is the most common copula verb.
5. indirect object: a noun or pronoun that comes between the verb and the direct object and identifies the 'to whom' or 'to what' of the direct object. I gave John an apple: gave an apple to whom? The answer is the indirect object. Other examples will vary.

Compose a sentence based upon each of the following criteria.
Answers will vary.

1. A simple sentence about Easter.
2. A compound sentence about Wales.
3. A complex sentence about cricket.
4. A complex sentence about Stonehenge.
5. A compound-complex sentence about breakfast.

2 Writing complete sentences

One-minute summary

The goal of this Chapter is to help you write complete sentences. To be complete, a sentence needs a subject and a verb, contained within a main or independent clause. Incomplete sentences are missing either a subject or a verb, possibly both, or contain a subject and a verb but within only a dependent or subordinate clause. Incomplete sentences are usually called sentence fragments. Under some circumstances, sentence fragments are acceptable, even effective. This Chapter provides definitions for and examples of the various types of sentence fragments and explains when sentence fragments are acceptable.

Sentence fragments caused by a missing subject or verb

Study carefully the following sentence.

> Fashion designers are influenced by the everyday clothing that people in their own country wear, but, in recent years, designers, especially those from Russia, have been looking for inspiration from the more exotic clothing traditionally worn by native people, the Maoris of New Zealand and the Zulus of South Africa, especially.

This is a correct, but long compound-complex sentence, and, in the interest of clarity, a writer might want to express this thought in two or even three separate sentences. There are several correct ways of doing so. Here is just one possibility.

> Fashion designers are influenced by the everyday clothing that people in their own country wear. In recent years, however, designers, especially those from Russia, have been looking for inspiration from

> the more exotic clothing traditionally worn by native people. They have been influenced, especially, by the clothing worn by the Maoris of New Zealand and the Zulus of South Africa.

What a writer needs to avoid, however, is breaking the long sentence up into sentence fragments.

> Fashion designers are influenced by the everyday clothing that people in their own country wear. Especially those from Russia. In recent years, however, designers have been looking for inspiration from the more exotic clothing traditionally worn by native people. For example, the Maoris of New Zealand and the Zulus of South Africa.

In this passage, the first sentence is fine. It has its subject—'fashion designers'—and its verb—'are influenced'. It continues with a prepositional phrase—'by the everyday clothing'—and a subordinate clause—'that people in their own country wear'—which has, within it, another prepositional phrase—'in their own country'. But look at the next word group, which is punctuated as if it were a sentence. It is not a sentence because it has neither a subject nor a verb. It is a sentence fragment. The third sentence is fine. It has its subject—'designers'—and its verb—'have been looking'—and the usual assortment of phrases and modifying words. The last word group has a subject, a compound subject, in fact—'Maoris and Zulus'. But the subjects are not doing anything; there is no verb; this is a sentence fragment. To correct it, the writer would have to add a verb:

> For example, the Maoris of New Zealand and the Zulus of South Africa have inspired fashion designers around the world.

The sentence fragment caused by a subordinate conjunction or a relative pronoun

You will recall from Chapter One that a group of words can contain a subject and a verb but still be less than a sentence.

Such word groups are called dependent or subordinate clauses, dependent because their meaning depends upon their partnership with a main clause (a complete sentence), subordinate because they are less than, subordinate to a complete sentence. Dependent clauses begin with subordinate conjunctions or relative pronouns. Common subordinate conjunctions include although, while, because, if, when, since, as, before, after. Common relative pronouns include who, whom, whose, that, and which. As a rule, dependent clauses that begin with a subordinate conjunction qualify verbs, and those that begin with a relative pronoun qualify nouns.

Notice, for example, what happens when we add a subordinate conjunction to a complete sentence:

> The quality of clothing manufactured in China is improving every year.
> While the quality of clothing manufactured in China is improving every year...
> Although the quality of clothing manufactured in China is improving every year...
> Since the quality of clothing manufactured in China is improving every year...
> If quality of clothing manufactured in China is improving every year...

The first sentence is complete, the other four are not; they are sentence fragments. The addition of the subordinate conjunction renders them subordinate to a main or independent clause. Less experienced writers often mistake subordinate clauses for complete sentences, especially when the subordinate clause follows the main clause:

> The quality of the clothing manufactured in Western Europe seems to be declining. While the quality of clothing manufactured in China is improving every year.
> The Chinese textile industry is stagnant. Although the quality of clothing manufactured in China is improving every year.

American consumers are spending more money in Chinese department stores. Since the quality of clothing manufactured in China is improving.

The Chinese fashion industry will become more profitable. If quality of clothing manufactured in China continues to improve.

In each example above, the second 'sentence' is not a sentence at all but a sentence fragment. The complete sentence should be followed by a comma, and the subordinate conjunctions (while, although, since, if) should begin with a lower-case letter.

Now look what happens when we add a relative pronoun to a complete sentence:

The Gothic look is popular among Chinese teenagers.

The Gothic look, which is popular among Chinese teenagers...

The look that is most popular among Chinese teenagers...

Again, the inclusion of the relative pronoun raises the reader's expectations, implying as it does that something else remains to be said. The first sentence is complete. The other two word groups are sentence fragments.

A digression: Which and that

Convention holds that the relative pronoun 'which' introduces a clause that is not essential to the meaning of a sentence, while 'that' introduces a clause that, if eliminated, would render the sentence vague, even meaningless. A clause not essential to the meaning of a sentence is sometimes called a 'non-restrictive clause'; one essential to the meaning of the sentence is called a 'restrictive clause'. A non-restrictive clause is preceded by a comma, while a restrictive clause is not. The distinction is apparent in these two sentences:

This season, some designers are showing the Gothic look, which is popular among Chinese teenagers.

> One look that is currently popular among Chinese teenagers is Gothic.
>
> If you eliminate the clause in the first sentence, you still have a sentence that makes sense, but if you eliminate the clause in the second sentence, the sentence loses essential meaning.
>
> And remember that the dependent clause must be attached to the independent clause or you will have a sentence fragment, as in this example:
>
> This season, some designers are showing the Gothic look. Which is popular among Chinese teenagers.

Here are other examples of sentence fragments which results from the misuse of a relative pronoun:

Handbags designed by Etienne Champlain are very popular among film stars. Who are among the few people who can afford to pay five hundred pounds for a purse.

All of the successful young film stars are carrying around those five-hundred-pound handbags. Which are designed by Etienne Champlain.

In both examples above, the main clause should be followed by a comma, and the relative pronouns (who and which) should begin with a lower-case letter.

When the sentence fragment is acceptable

Here are the first three 'sentences' of Charles Dickens' famous novel *Bleak House.*

> London. Michaelmas term lately over, and the Lord Chancellor sitting in Lincoln's Inn Hall. Implacable November weather.

Each of these 'sentences' is incomplete; each is a sentence fragment. The first is a single noun without a verb. The second needs the verb 'is' (or 'was') before the word 'sitting' to make it complete. The third consists of an adjective, followed by a noun-adjective, followed by a noun; it also has no verb. But, obviously, this writing is not wrong or incorrect. Dickens is using fragments deliberately to help set the bleak mood of his novel, to help convey the impression of a London with something essential missing.

It is acceptable for writers to write incomplete sentences when they are doing so for a particular effect, which is often to achieve emphasis or to establish a particular tone. Dickens continues the first chapter of *Bleak House* with one fragment after another. Here are just a few.

Dogs, undistinguishable in mire.
Fog everywhere.
Fog on the Essex marshes, fog on the Kentish heights.

Here are some other, less literary, examples of sentence fragments, which might be acceptable because the writers use them deliberately to achieve a rhetorical effect.

On Thursday, he wrote the exam and this time he passed. <u>At last</u>. <u>At long last.</u>

<u>Never</u>. He did not say as much, but the president knew that was when he would re-appoint see the general.

The electricity went out, the reservoir froze, and the paper said the storm would rage for two, maybe three more days. <u>A very disturbing sequence of events, especially for the poor residents of the city.</u>

Heed this warning, though: if you are a student, writing a paper or a report for your teacher or professor, you are wise to avoid sentence fragments, even if you know you are writing an incomplete sentence and are doing so for a particular effect. Your teacher might not see it as effective and might deduct a point for an error.

Tutorial

Progress questions

Re-write the following passages to correct any sentence fragments.

1. If you live in London and own a weekend home in the country, you will spend half of that weekend on the motorway. Not the most efficient use of time. Still, many affluent families are buying cottages in the country. Though they are buying them as much as investments as places to escape for a holiday. And renting them out.
2. There are many cottages for rent in the Cotswolds. In fact, about 5% of the houses in the Cotswolds are available for rent throughout the year. Or at certain times throughout the year. The Cotswolds are especially popular because of the scenic rolling countryside. And the proximity to London.
3. Renting a Cotswold cottage for a weekend in the country in the summer is expensive. Almost £1500 per average. But the cost usually includes a well-stocked fridge and larder and transportation. If you enjoy riding a bicycle. And they often feature swimming pools, gyms, and playgrounds for children. Sometimes even a spa where you can get a massage, a facial, a manicure or any combination thereof.
4. Christie's estimated that the black dress that Audrey Hepburn wore in *Breakfast at Tiffany's* would fetch between fifty and seventy thousand pounds at auction. Try six times that amount. The battle was between three bidders. Two in the room and one on the phone. None of the three was willing to back down. At least not until the bidding reached four hundred thousand pounds. At which point, one of the bidders dropped out. A second refused to go beyond the £467,000 that the dress eventually sold for. To the amazement of the audience.
5. The designer of the dress was Hubert de Givenchy. He gave it to a charity devoted to combating poverty in India. Because he knew Audrey Hepburn was a great humanitarian, determined to use her fame as a way to help others.

She wore the dress in the opening scene of *Breakfast at Tiffany's*. In which she played eccentric Manhattan socialite Holly Golightly.

Define and provide, in a sentence, an example of the following terms:

1. subordinate conjunction
2. relative pronoun
3. subordinate clause
4. independent clause
5. acceptable sentence fragment.

Discussion point

Why will you see the occasional sentence fragment when you read a book or your favourite newspapers or magazines?

Practical assignment

Review written work that you have done in the past, check to see if there are any sentence fragments in that work, and correct them, if there are.

Study and revision tip

Read your written work out loud before you turn it in to be graded or published. Listen for word groups that might not be complete sentences and revise them accordingly.

Answers to the progress questions

Re-write the following passages to correct any sentence fragments.

Note that there are many ways to correct these passages. The versions below are the same as above, but the sentence fragments have been underlined.

1. If you live in London and own a weekend home in the country, you will spend half of that weekend on the motorway. <u>Not the most efficient use of time</u>. Still, many affluent families are buying cottages in the country. <u>Though they are buying them as much as investments as places to escape for a holiday</u>. <u>And renting them out.</u>

2. There are many cottages for rent in the Cotswolds. In fact, about 5% of the houses in the Cotswolds are available for rent throughout the year. Or at certain times throughout the year. The Cotswolds are especially popular because of the scenic rolling countryside. And the proximity to London.
3. Renting a Cotswold cottage for a weekend in the country in the summer is expensive. Almost £1500 per average. But the cost usually includes a well-stocked fridge and larder and transportation. If you enjoy riding a bicycle. And they often feature swimming pools, gyms, and playgrounds for children. Sometimes even a spa where you can get a massage, a facial, a manicure or any combination thereof.
4. Christie's estimated that the black dress that Audrey Hepburn wore in *Breakfast at Tiffany's* would fetch between fifty and seventy thousand pounds at auction. Try six times that amount. The battle was between three bidders. Two in the room and one on the phone. None of the three was willing to back down. At least not until the bidding reached four hundred thousand pounds. At which point, one of the bidders dropped out. A second refused to go beyond the £467,000 that the dress eventually sold for. To the amazement of the audience.
5. The designer of the dress was Hubert de Givenchy. He gave it to a charity devoted to combating poverty in India. Because he knew Audrey Hepburn was a great humanitarian, determined to use her fame as a way to help others. She wore the dress in the opening scene of *Breakfast at Tiffany's*. In which she played eccentric Manhattan socialite Holly Golightly.

Define and provide an example of the following terms.

Note that the definitions are included below but not the sentences, which will vary.

1. Subordinate conjunction: a word that introduces a subordinate (or dependent) clause, usually one that will qualify a verb.
2. Relative pronoun: also a word that introduces a subordinate clause, but usually one that will qualify a noun.

3. Subordinate clause: also known as a dependent clause, a group of words that cannot stand alone as a sentence, even though the word group does include a subject and a verb.
4. Independent clause: also known as a main clause and synonymous with a complete sentence; a group of words that contains a subject and a verb and that stand alone as a complete sentence.
5. Acceptable sentence fragment: a group of words that conforms to the definition of a sentence fragment but which is acceptable because the writer is using it for a particular rhetorical effect, especially emphasis.

3 Avoiding run-on sentences

One-minute summary

In Chapter Two, you learned how to distinguish between a complete and incomplete sentence, specifically how to avoid writing sentence fragments. In a sense, this Chapter deals with the opposite problem: how to avoid punctuating two sentences as if they are one, how, in other words, to avoid a run-on sentence. This error is usually caused when a writer uses a comma as if it were a stronger punctuation mark than it actually is, as if it were strong enough to separate two independent clauses, when, in fact, it is not. For this reason, this type of run-on sentence is called a comma splice or comma fault. Occasionally a writer will omit all punctuation between two independent clauses. This type of run-on sentence is called a fused sentence. This Chapter explains what run-on sentences are and provides you with strategies for recognising and avoiding them. Most important, it explains the three ways in which run-on sentences can be corrected, by using a coordinate conjunction, the correct punctuation, or a subordinate clause.

Correcting a run-on sentence by adding a coordinate conjunction

In Chapter Two, you learned that there are four types of sentences in the English language: simple, compound, complex, and compound-complex. In this Chapter, the compound and compound-complex sentences are especially important because these are the sentence types writers often punctuate, incorrectly, as run-on sentences. A compound sentence, you will recall, consists of two simple sentences (also known as independent or main clauses) joined together, correctly, to form one sentence. A compound-complex sentence adds a subordinate (also called a dependent) clause to the mix. A run-on sentence results when the two sentences are not joined together appropriately.

One way to correct a run-on sentence is to use a coordinate conjunction. A coordinate conjunction is a short word—and, but, or—that, along with a comma, connects together independent clauses. Here are two independent clauses, that is, two complete sentences:

> Orbiting spacecraft have confirmed that there is ice at the poles of Mars. Water must be present to sustain life on the Red Planet.

Clearly, these two sentences have a rhetorical connection, and, therefore, they could be linked together to form a single sentence. It would <u>not</u> be correct to link these two sentences together with a comma only. This would result in a run-on sentence, also called a comma splice or a comma fault:

> Orbiting spacecraft have confirmed that there is ice at the poles of Mars, water must be present to sustain life on the Red Planet.

It would be acceptable, however, to place a coordinate conjunction before the comma. Clearly, the logical coordinate conjunction to choose for this sentence would be 'but'.

> Orbiting spacecraft have confirmed that there is ice at the poles of Mars, but water must be present to sustain life on the Red Planet.

Here are two more examples of run-on sentences, followed by the same sentences corrected by the inclusion of a coordinate conjunction, which is underlined.

> NASA's Mars Global Surveyor spacecraft captured new, sharper images of Mars, some of these images show gullies with deposits likely left by flowing water.
>
> The water might have bubbled up from below the ground, it might have come from melted ice.

> NASA's Mars Global Surveyor spacecraft captured new, sharper images of Mars, <u>and some</u> of these

images show gullies with deposits likely left by flowing water.

The water might have bubbled up from below the ground, or it might have come from melted ice.

Note that each of the example sentences used so far contains two complete independent clauses, as a compound sentence must. If you write a sentence that has two verbs that have the same subject, you no longer have a compound sentence. You have a simple sentence, and you may, therefore, eliminate the comma. In this sentence, for example, the comma is necessary:

The Mars Global Surveyor spacecraft orbited Mars for ten years, but it lost contact with mission control in November of 2006.

But, in the sentence above, the second subject 'it' can be eliminated because it refers to the first subject 'spacecraft'. If 'it' is eliminated, though, the sentence is no longer a compound but a simple sentence with two verbs. Therefore, the comma should be eliminated, as well:

The Mars Global Surveyor spacecraft orbited Mars for ten years but lost contact with mission control in November of 2006.

A digression: The conjunctive adverb

Less experienced writers often confuse coordinate conjunctions with conjunctive adverbs. Like a coordinate conjunction, a conjunctive adverb can link two sentences together. A conjunctive adverb is a word which establishes a rhetorical relationship between two sentences by signaling a contradiction, an addition, or a qualification. 'However', 'nevertheless', 'therefore', and 'consequently' are common conjunctive adverbs. Some coordinate conjunctions and conjunctive adverbs are similar in meaning, for example 'but' and 'however'. But, unlike a coordinate conjunction, a conjunctive adverb cannot be used with a comma to separate two complete sentences. This sentence, for example, is a run-on:

The Mars Global Surveyor spacecraft orbited Mars for ten years, however it lost contact with mission control in November of 2006.

To correct this run-on sentence, you could put a period after 'years' and capitalise 'however'. Since there is a close rhetorical relationship between the two sentences, you could also use a semi-colon before 'however'. Convention also dictates that a comma then follows the conjunctive adverb:

The Mars Global Surveyor spacecraft orbited Mars for ten years; however, it lost contact with mission control in November of 2006.
The Mars Global Surveyor spacecraft orbited Mars for ten years. However, it lost contact with mission control in November of 2006.

Of course, if the conjunctive adverb is used within as opposed to at the beginning of the sentence, it is preceded and followed by a comma.

The Mars Global Surveyor spacecraft orbited Mars for ten years. It lost contact with mission control, however, in November of 2006.

Here are two more compound sentences that use a conjunctive adverb as their link:

Water has likely flowed on the surface of Mars within the past five years; consequently, there may be life on the Red Planet.
It is not likely that there are micro-organisms frozen in water deposits below the surface of Mars; nevertheless, that possibility does exist.

Correcting a run-on sentence by using punctuation

Earlier in this Chapter, you learned that a comma is not a strong enough punctuation mark to use between two complete sentences. There are, however, three punctuation marks that are strong enough. Obviously, a period can be used to separate sentences. But, as you may recall from Chapter One, a colon or a semi-colon may also be used, depending on the rhetorical relationship of the two independent clauses. If the two clauses are related semantically, then a semi-colon can connect them:

> Nintendo sold 50,000 units of its new gaming console the Wii, in the first twelve hours it was on sale; that translates to about one unit every second.

Note that if the writer had used a comma instead of a semi-colon, he would have written a run-on sentence.

If the second sentence explains or elaborates upon a point from the first, you may use a colon:

> The Wii is not a bargain: it sells for £179.99.

Note that if the writer had used a comma instead of the colon, he would have written a run-on sentence.

Correcting a run-on sentence using a subordinate conjunction

You can also correct a run-on sentence by reducing one of the independent clauses to a dependent clause, using a subordinate conjunction. Study how these run-on sentences have been corrected. The subordinate conjunction is underlined.

> The console has won rave reviews, it comes with a want that replicates on screen the players' hand and arm movements.
>
> The console has won rave reviews, because it comes with a want that replicates on screen the players' hand and arm movements.

> Nintendo is manufacturing new Wiis as quickly as it can, the company is looking to hire more skilled workers.
>
> If Nintendo can find the skilled workers it needs, the company will manufacture new Wiis as quickly as it can.

> Wii users are smashing vases and even television sets in the rooms where they are gaming, they lose

their grip on the controller and it crashes into other objects.

Wii users are smashing vases and even television sets in the rooms where they are gaming, <u>when</u> they lose their grip on the controller and it crashes into other objects.

Remember, from Chapter Two, that it would not be acceptable to use a semi-colon or a period between the dependent and the independent clauses in the above sentences because the dependent clause would then become a sentence fragment.

Correcting a run-on sentence using a relative pronoun

You can also correct a run-on sentence by reducing one of the independent clauses to a dependent clause, using a relative pronoun. Study how these run-on sentences have been corrected. The relative pronoun is underlined.

Nintendo has released its Wii before its arch rival Sony releases its PlayStation 3, PS3 will not be released until March.

Nintendo has released its Wii before its arch rival Sony releases its PlayStation 3, <u>which</u> will not be released until March.

Customers, mainly young men, spent £180 for the Wii, many of the same young men will be determined to find the £425 they will need to purchase the PlayStation 3!

Many of the same young men <u>who</u> spent £180 for the Wii will be determined to find the £425 they will need to purchase the PlayStation 3!

Correcting a run-on sentence by using a phrase

You can also correct a run-on sentence by reducing one of the independent clauses to a phrase. A phrase, you will recall from Chapter One, is a group of words that does not contain a subject or a verb and modifies a word, usually a noun or a verb in a sentence. Here are two run-on sentences, corrected by reducing one of the independent clauses to a phrase:

PlayStation 3 will appeal to computer game fanatics, they are willing to pay whatever it costs for the latest technology.
PlayStation 3 will appeal to computer game fanatics, willing to pay whatever it costs for the latest technology.

Microsoft also has a new computer game, the Xbox 360, it was launched at the end of 2005.
Microsoft also has a new computer game, the Xbox 360, launched at the end of 2005.

There are, then, three ways to correct a run-on sentence. You can add a coordinate conjunction to the comma; replace the comma with a stronger punctuation mark—a period, a semi-colon, or a colon—; or you can reduce one of the independent clauses to a phrase or to a dependent clause by using either a relative pronoun or a subordinate conjunction. Here is one final example of a run-on sentence, followed by a variety of sentences, correctly revised:

Young men work the console of a video game with the skill of a surgeon performing a delicate operation, most adults older than thirty work the console as if it were Rubik's cube.

Young men work the console of a video game with the skill of a surgeon performing a delicate operation, but most adults older than thirty work the console as if it were Rubik's cube.
Young men work the console of a video game with the skill of a surgeon performing a delicate operation, while most adults older than thirty work the console as if it were Rubik's cube.
While young men work the console of a video game with the skill of a surgeon performing a delicate

operation, most adults older than thirty work the console as if it were Rubik's cube.

Young men work the console of a video game with the skill of a surgeon performing a delicate operation; however, most adults older than thirty work the console as if it were Rubik's cube.

Young men, who work the console of a video game with the skill of a surgeon performing a delicate operation, are more adept than most adults older than thirty, who work the console as if were is Rubik's cube.

Tutorial

Progress questions

Re-write the following passages to correct any run-on sentences.

1. Ice in the Arctic is melting very rapidly, expert climatologists claim it will all be gone in thirty years.
2. Carbon emissions are heating the earth, they form a smog barrier which prevents heat from escaping into the atmosphere.
3. Some ice would remain on the coasts of Greenland and Ellesmere Island, the rest of the Arctic Ocean will be open water.
4. Climatologists with the British Antarctic Survey believe the arctic ice will disappear even more rapidly, their satellites show images that indicate the arctic ice is melting at a rate almost twice as fast as the rate predicted by the NASA-funded US team of researchers.
5. Ice reflects heat, as the ice disappears the amount of heat it reflects away from the earth diminishes.

Define and provide, in a sentence, an example of the following terms:

1. coordinate conjunction
2. conjunctive adverb
3. fused sentence
4. colon (the punctuation mark)
5. semi-colon.

Discussion point

Are there more ways to correct a sentence fragment or a run-on sentence?

Practical assignment

Review written work that you have done in the past, check to see if there are any run-on sentences in that work, and correct them if there are.

Study and revision tip

Remember to learn all three ways to correct a run-on sentence.

Answers to the progress questions

Re-write the following passages to correct any run-on sentences.

Note that the corrections below represent just one of several ways these sentences can be corrected.

1. Ice in the Arctic is melting very rapidly, and expert climatologists claim it will all be gone in thirty years.
2. Carbon emissions, which form a smog barrier that prevents heat from escaping into the atmosphere, are heating the earth.
3. Some ice would remain on the coasts of Greenland and Ellesmere Island; however, the rest of the Arctic Ocean will be open water.
4. Climatologists with the British Antarctic Survey believe the arctic ice will disappear even more rapidly, because their satellites show images that indicate the arctic ice is melting at a rate almost twice as fast as the rate predicted by the NASA-funded US team of researchers.
5. Since ice reflects heat, as the ice disappears, the amount of heat it reflects away from the earth diminishes.

Define and provide an example of the following terms.

Note that the definitions are included below but not the sentences, which will vary.

1. coordinate conjunction: small word (most common ones are and, but, or) which combines with a comma to separate two independent clauses.
2. conjunctive adverb: a word (common ones include because, if, when, since, although) which introduces a dependent clause, usually one that qualifies a verb.
3. fused sentence: two independent clauses incorrectly joined together without punctuation or a linking word between them.

4. colon (the punctuation mark): a punctuation mark consisting of one dot below another dot; separates two independent clauses when the second elaborates upon or explains something about the first.
5. semi-colon: a punctuation mark consisting of a dot above a comma; separates two independent clauses about the same subject.

4 Writing clear sentences

One-minute summary

Sentence fragments (the subject of Chapter Two) and run-on sentences (the subject of Chapter Three) can confuse readers because they break the rules of sentence boundaries: fragments are incomplete; run-ons are two sentences masquerading as one. There are other common errors in sentence structure that can impair clarity. They are:

- Faulty parallelism
- Misplaced and dangling modifiers
- Shifts in voice and point-of-view
- Faulty predication.

Writers need to recognise and avoid these errors or correct them when they are proofreading their work and realise they have written an incorrect sentence. This Chapter explains these errors in sentence structure and teaches you how to recognise, avoid, and correct them.

Recognising and avoiding faulty parallelism

If a sentence has more than one word, phrase, or clause modifying or working in conjunction with the same word within the sentence, those words, phrases, and clauses should be rhetorically equal. If they are not, that sentence is not parallel. Consider this sentence:

> Opponents of Augusto Pinochet insist he seized power by force, curtailed democratic freedoms, and was torturing his political enemies.

Note that the subject 'he' has three verbs, 'seized', 'curtailed' and 'was torturing'. All three of these verbs should be rhetorically equal because they are all serving the same function. But they are not all rhetorically equal in the sentence above: Two end in 'ed' and one in 'ing'. This is the error known as 'faulty parallelism' because one of the three verbs is not in a parallel relationship with the other two. The sentence needs to be correct, either by changing the 'ing' verb into an 'ed' verb:

> Opponents of Augusto Pinochet insist he seized power by force, curtailed democratic freedoms, and tortured his political enemies.

> Or you may change the two 'ed' verbs into an 'ing' verb:

> Opponents of Augusto Pinochet accused him of seizing power by force, curtailing democratic freedoms, and torturing his political enemies.

Here are three more examples of faulty parallelism, followed by correct sentences:

> Supporters of Augusto Pinochet claim he saved the country from communist tyranny, political corruption, and an economy that would have lacked stability.
>
> Supporters of Augusto Pinochet claim he saved the country from communist tyranny, political corruption, and economic instability.

> Pinochet was born in 1915, ruled Chile from 1973 to 1990, and his heart failed in 2006, resulting in his death.
>
> Pinochet was born in 1915, ruled Chile from 1973 to 1990, and died from heart failure in 2006.

> Pinochet claimed he deposed his predecessor, socialist president Salvadore Allende, because Allende was destroying the Chilean economy by nationalizing private industry and journalists who were critical of his policies were threatened with imprisonment.
>
> Pinochet claimed he deposed his predecessor, socialist president Salvadore Allende, because

> Allende was destroying the Chilean economy by nationalizing private industry and was threatening to imprison journalists critical of his policies.

Recognising and avoiding misplaced and dangling modifiers

Adjectives and adverbs, as single words, as phrases, or as clauses, modify or qualify other words in a sentence. Adjectives usually modify nouns; adverbs modify verbs, adjectives, or other adverbs. These modifying words can often be used in different places within a sentence. Notice, for example, how the adverb 'slowly' may be placed in these sentences:

> Slowly, he walked toward me.
> He walked slowly toward me.
> He walked toward me slowly.
> He slowly walked toward me.

And notice how the adjectives 'cold and wet' may be used in these sentences:

> Cold and wet, the puppy found his way home.
> The puppy, cold and wet, found his way home.
> The cold, wet puppy found his way home.

But modifiers cannot be placed anywhere within a sentence. Their relationship to the word they are modifying must be clear. They cannot appear to modify a word other than the word the writer means them to modify. Consider this sentence:

> The Kalahari Bushmen sued the Botswana government, with the support of Survival International, accusing it of evicting them from their homeland illegally.

Who, in this sentence, has the support of Survival International? The placement of the two phrases 'with the support of Survival International' suggests that the government has their support. But surely the intent of the sentence is to indicate that Survival International is on the side of the Bushmen: they are the ones being evicted, the ones in need of survival. Those phrases are misplaced. They form a misplaced modifier. Put them at the beginning of the sentence and see what happens:

> With the support of Survival International, The Kalahari Bushmen sued the Botswana government, accusing it of evicting them from their homeland illegally.

Now it is clear that the Bushmen, not the government, have the support of Survival International. Notice, as well, that it is also clearer now that the pronoun 'it' refers to the government and 'them' refers to the Bushmen.

Here is another example:

> Bringing to an end the country's longest-running court case, the Bushmen got a favourable ruling from Botswana's High Court and will soon return to live and hunt in the Kalahari Desert.

Who brought the country's longest-running court case to an end? The sentence seems to imply that the Bushmen did, but surely the writer means that the High Court did. That phrase 'Bringing to an end the country's longest-running court case' dangles at the beginning of the sentence, waiting for its partner, which does not arrive for seven more words, by which time, the reader might be confused. This is the error known as the dangling modifier, also called the unattached participle. To correct the error, the writer needs to get the High Court closer to the case on which it ruled:

> Bringing to an end the country's longest-running court case, the High Court of Botswana ruled in favour of the Bushmen, who will soon return to live and hunt in the Kalahari Desert.

Here is another sentence that contains a misplaced modifier, followed by an explanation for why it is misplaced, followed by another sentence, which places the modifier correctly.

> The De Beers Corporation conspired with the government to evict the Bushmen so it could mine

> the Kalahari Desert, according to lawyers for the Bushmen, believed to be rich in diamonds.

Who or what is 'rich in diamonds'? The writer wants to say the Kalahari Desert is, but seems to indicate the lawyers and/or the Bushmen are. The writer needs to change the position of the modifier so it is clear it refers to the Desert.

> According to lawyers for the Bushmen, the De Beers Corporation conspired with the government to evict the Bushmen so it could mine the Kalahari Desert, believed to be rich in diamonds.

Here is another sentence that contains a dangling modifier, followed by an explanation for why it dangles, followed by another sentence, with the error corrected.

> Having compensated the Bushmen for the land they lost, the wildlife of the Central Kalahari, especially the endangered species, should no longer be hunted.

Who compensated the Bushmen for their lost land? The sentence does not say, though it seems to imply the wildlife suddenly became uncharacteristically generous. The writer wants to say the government compensated the Bushmen but left out that important detail. The sentence needs to be revised, along these lines:

> The Government, having compensated the Bushmen for the land they lost, has protected the wildlife of the Central Kalahari, especially the endangered species, which should no longer be hunted.

Recognising and avoiding ambiguous shifts

Another enemy of sentence clarity is a jarring change within a sentence in point-of-view, verb tense, or purpose.

Here is a sentence within which the shift in point-of-view could cause confusion.

> In 1998, we paid £240 for a case Chateau Lafite Rothschild, which would cost you £2,370 today.

The point of view in this sentence begins as the first-person plural 'we' then shifts to the second person 'you'. It's somewhat confusing, suggesting as it could that 'we' would still pay the same today, whereas 'you' would have to pay more. The sentence is clearer if the point-of-view is consistent.

> In 1998, we paid £1,240 for a case Chateau Lafite Rothschild, which would cost <u>us</u> £2,370 today.

<u>Verb tense</u> often changes in the course of a sentence to indicate the temporal context of the sentence's action. Consider this sentence:

> Chateau Lafite Rothschild is the claret by which others are measured, and, because it soared in price last month, other clarets will also increase in value.

This sentence begins with the present tense verb 'is', then switches to past 'are measured' and 'soared', and then switches again to future 'will increase'. It must do so to establish the temporal relationships among what is happening now, what happened 'last month' and what will happen in the future. (Note that verb tense is discussed in detail in Chapter Seven.) But if the temporal relationships do not change, the verb tense should not change. Here is a sentence with a jarring shift in verb tense:

> Fine wine is excellent investment, which often outperformed stocks and bonds.

In this sentence the shift to the past 'outperformed' is unnecessary and confusing. Here, consistency ensures clarity:

> Fine wine is excellent investment, which often outperforms stocks and bonds.

Here is another example of a sentence within which a shift in verb tense might be confusing; it is followed by a revised version.

> Oversized sunglasses, in shapes and colours that Audrey Hepburn and Jackie Kennedy used to wear,

are coming back in style, and manufacturers increase production to meet the demand.

This sentence contains three verbs. The first, 'used to wear', is appropriately in past tense, since Audrey Hepburn and Jackie Kennedy no longer wear oversized or any other sunglasses. The other two verbs, though, must be consistent in tense because they accompany the same subject 'sunglasses'. The verb 'are coming' is in progressive tense, while the verb 'increase' is in present tense. To avoid the unnecessary shift, the writer needs to change 'increase' to progressive:

> Oversized sunglasses, in shapes and colours that Audrey Hepburn and Jackie Kennedy used to wear, are coming back in style, and manufacturers are increasing production to meet the demand.

Be wary, also, of a shift in purpose within a single sentence. It is acceptable to make a statement and ask a question in the same sentence, if the question suggests the statement will be contradicted.

> Women are visiting tanning salons in the winter to prevent their summer glow from fading, but are those tanning bed lights harmful to the skin?

But avoid shifting the purpose of your sentence from a statement to a question if the question implies support for the statement. Consider this sentence:

> Many dermatologists are concerned about the risks associated with tanning beds, and are their patients spending too much time under their harmful lights?

Because this sentence expresses the dermatologists' parallel concerns, its purpose should not shift. The sentence is more effective when the two parts are framed as parallel concerns:

> Many dermatologists are concerned about the risks associated with tanning beds, and worry that their patients are spending too much time under their harmful lights.

Similarly, a shift in a single sentence from an indirect to a direct quote can impair clarity. Consider this sentence:

> The *Star*'s fashion editor insisted the silver gown washed out the starlet's already pale skin, and promised she would urge Ms. Peters, please do not wear that dress again, until you are well tanned.

The first part of this sentence (ending with the first comma) reports on what the fashion editor said, but the last part (after the second comma) shifts the purpose from indirect to direct address, as the shift in pronoun from 'she' to 'you' implies. The sentence would be more effective if the purpose is consistent, which it would be if the case of the pronoun remained consistent.

> The *Star*'s fashion editor insisted the silver gown washed out the starlet's already pale skin, and promised she would urge Ms. Peters not to wear that dress again, until she is well tanned.

Recognising and avoiding wordiness

A good sentence is lean and muscular, not fat and padded. There are several mistakes inexperienced writers sometimes make that create wordy sentences: They repeat a word unnecessarily, they add adverbs and adjectives where such modifiers are not necessary, and they reiterate one thought or idea twice. Here are three examples of wordy sentences, followed by a leaner, more effective version of each.

> There is much dispute about where and when an ice hockey game was first played, with some sports historians claiming confidently that hockey was first played in Montreal at McGill University and other sports historians claiming Toronto as the birthplace of Canada's national sport and others insisting it was played in Windor Ontario before it was played in Montreal or Toronto.
>
> Sports historians dispute the location of the first ice hockey game, some claiming it was first played at McGill University in Montreal, others claiming

Toronto and still others insisting Windor, Ontario was the birthplace of Canada's national sport.

The nature of education is changing now that students can sit at home in front of a computer and watch and listen to their teacher's lessons and communicate via email with their teacher and with other students at the same time together or individually during online discussions and submit their assignments electronically and even take their course examinations.

Education is changing, now that students can watch and listen to their teacher's lessons, exchange group or individual emails with their teacher and classmates, submit their assignments, even write examinations, while they sit at home in front of their computers.

At one time, twenty or thirty years ago nutritionists scoffed at the claims of eighteenth-century coffee drinkers who believed in their writings that coffee was good for their health, but recent studies on the effect of moderate coffee consumption suggest that coffee, consumed in moderation which usually means about three to four cups a day, has health benefits in that drinking coffee may reduce the risk of colon and liver cancer, delay the onset of diabetes, alleviate the symptoms of cirrhosis of the liver, primarily because brewed coffee is a fine source of concentration of anti-oxidants, having about four times the amount of anti-oxidants as green tea.

Nutritionists used to scoff at those eighteenth-century coffee drinkers who wrote about the health benefits of coffee, but recent studies, on the effects of consuming three or four cups of coffee a day, suggest that moderate coffee consumption may reduce the risk of colon and liver cancer, delay the onset of diabetes, and alleviate the symptoms of cirrhosis of the liver, primarily because coffee is an excellent source of anti-oxidants, four times better than green tea.

A digression: Passive voice

Passive voice is a verb form which consists of one form of the verb 'to be' followed by the past participle of a main verb, a construction which occurs in sentences wherein the natural object becomes the subject. If the sentence 'Many young girls play football' was re-written as 'Football is played by many young girls', an active-voice sentence would become passive. Note that in shifting from the active to the passive voice, the word length of the sentence increases from five to seven and the style of the sentence seems to less natural. For this reason, many editors and teachers advise against the use of passive voice, on the grounds that it creates a wordy and awkward sentence.

When this is true, as it is in our example above, you should avoid passive voice. In some sentences, however, the subject is indeterminate or superfluous and passive voice is quite acceptable: 'Smoking is forbidden on all flights' is an acceptable alternative for 'Federal law prohibits smoking on all flights' or 'The management of Sun Airlines forbids smoking on all flights'.

For some writing assignments, convention dictates the use of passive voice. Reporting on an experiment, for example, scientists tend to prefer the passive 'Three milligrams of nitrogen were added to the solution' to the active 'We added three milligrams of nitrogen to the solution', because it is the experiment and its outcome, not their participation in it that they wish to highlight.

Recognising and avoiding faulty predication

Consider this sentence:

> Chinese law prohibits one child only for married couples.

The predicate of this sentence, which consists of the verb 'prohibits' plus the words and phrases which modify it—'one child only for married couples'—does not follow from the sentence's subject 'law'. The law prohibits married couples from having more than one child; to indicate it prohibits one child does not make sense. In other words, the predicate of this sentence is out of sync with its subject, creating the error known as faulty predication. The sentence needs to be revised to clarify the relationship between the sentence's subject and its predicate:

> Chinese law prohibits married couples from having more than one child.

Here is another example:

> Surveys conducted by social scientists in China suggest that the country has created a family planning policy of a generation of indulged and undisciplined children.

The meaning of this sentence is muddled because the predicate that follows the subject 'country' does not make clear that it is the government's policy and not the government itself that has created the generation of indulged and undisciplined children. The predicate needs to be revised to clarify the true nature of the relationship between that subject and its predicate:

> Surveys conducted by social scientists in China suggest that the country's family planning policy has created a generation of indulged and undisciplined children.

The revised sentence makes it clear that government policy, but not the country itself, has created a problem.

Tutorial

Progress questions

Re-write the following sentences to clarify their meaning.

1. Results of a recent survey suggest that more than half of the sixteen-year-old girls living in London and Birmingham are sexually active without condoms or other forms of birth control.
2. Using birth control is a precaution young, unmarried couples who are sexually active use.
3. Pablo Picasso is an internationally famous painter and he sculpted, but he also wrote a little-known play call *Desire Caught by the Tail.*
4. A Spaniard, the play by Picasso will be staged in his native country for the first-time since 1944, at which time it was put on in Paris by some of Picasso's famous friends, including Jean-Paul Sartre and Albert Camus.
5. The play is difficult to produce because it is surrealistic, it has no plot, and its convoluted dialogue is difficult for the actors to memorise.
6. The action of *Desire Caught by the Tail* takes place in a single room in Paris, while that city was being occupied by the Nazis, and it tells the story of a group of artists who are trying to cope with the Nazi occupation by eating and drinking to excess, sexual promiscuous behaviour, and reading and writing poetry.
7. After reading one of Picasso's plays, stick to painting was the advice American writer Gertrude Stein offered to Picasso.
8. Caffeine acts as a mild stimulant to the central nervous system which interferes with the production of adenosine, which induces sleep and which is why the caffeine in coffee keeps us awake.
9. Some studies suggest that caffeine can decrease muscle pain, alleviate the symptoms of asthma, and boost athletic performance, but it should be consumed in moderation.
10. A California sociologist examined thousands of death certificates and found that men whose initials spelled out

a word with negative connotations such as D.I.E. or P.I.G. were more likely to die when they were younger and to die by committing suicide than men were whose initials spelled out a word with more positive connotations such as A.C.E. or V.I.P, though the difference might have as much to do with treatment from parents who would lay such a moniker on their children than the difference has to do with the initials themselves.

Define and provide, in a sentence, an example of the following terms:

1. dangling modifier
2. misplaced modifier
3. faulty predication
4. passive voice
5. parallelism.

Discussion point

When is the use of passive voice acceptable, even preferable?

Practical assignment

Read carefully today's issue of your local newspaper and see if you can spot any sentences which could be revised to improve their clarity.

Study and revision tip

During one of the three or four times you might revise your written work, concentrate <u>only</u> on sentence clarity.

Answers to the progress questions

Re-write the following sentences to clarify their meaning.

Note that the corrections below represent just one of several ways these sentences can be corrected.

1. Results of a recent survey suggest that more than half of the sixteen-year-old girls living in London and Birmingham are sexually active but do not use birth control or insist their partners wear a condom.

2. Unmarried couples who are sexually active use should use birth control.
3. Pablo Picasso is an internationally famous painter and sculptor, but he also wrote a little-known play call *Desire Caught by the Tail.*
4. The play by Picasso will be produced in his native Spain for the first-time since 1944, when it was staged in Paris by some of Picasso's famous friends, including Jean-Paul Sartre and Albert Camus.
5. The play is difficult to produce because it is surrealistic, it has no plot, and it uses convoluted dialogue, difficult for the actors to memorise.
6. The action of *Desire Caught by the Tail* takes place in a single room in Paris, while that city was being occupied by the Nazis, and it tells the story of a group of artists who are trying to cope with the Nazi occupation by eating and drinking to excess, engaging in sexual promiscuity, and reading and writing poetry.
7. After reading one of Picasso's plays, to stick painting. American writer Gertrude Stein to Picasso.
8. Caffeine acts as a mild stimulant to the central nervous system which interferes with the production of adenosine, which induces sleep. For this reason caffeine in coffee keeps us awake.
9. Some studies suggest that, caffeine consumed in moderation can decrease muscle pain, alleviate the symptoms of asthma, and boost athletic performance.
10. A California sociologist examined thousands of death certificates and found that men whose initials spelled out a word with negative connotations such as D.I.E. or P.I.G. were more likely to die young and to die by committing suicide than were men whose initials spelled out a word with more positive connotations such as A.C.E. or V.I.P.. The difference thouth might have as much to do with treatment from parents who would lay such a moniker on their children than the difference has to do with the initials themselves.

Define and provide an example of the following terms.

Note that the definitions are included below but not the sentences, which will vary.

1. dangling modifier: often at the beginning of a sentence, a word or phrase causing confusion by modifying an absent or distant word.
2. misplaced modifier: a word, phrase, or clause so far away from the word it modifies that the entire sentence is rendered unclear.
3. faulty predication: a sentence whose predicate does not seem to match with its subject.
4. passive voice: form of verb resulting from the use of a form of the verb 'to be' plus the past participle of another verb.
5. parallelism: in rhetoric denotes a series of words, phrases, or clauses that begin with the same part of speech.

5 Pronoun reference and agreement

One-minute summary

Pronouns are short words—I, me, you, her, she, he, his, her, they, their, them—which take the place of a noun, so the noun does not have to be repeated unnecessarily often. Writers must be careful, however, to make certain it is clear exactly what noun it is that the pronoun is replacing because one sentence might contain several nouns and pronouns. Similarly, some pronouns—she, he, his, her—signal gender, while many nouns—manager, athlete, doctor—do not, so it is also important gender-specific nouns are avoided when referring to gender-neutral nouns. In this Chapter, you will learn to:

- Avoid using pronouns ambiguously
- Avoid using gender specific pronouns inappropriately.

Avoiding ambiguous pronouns

Consider this sentence:

> Allison is tall and slender, and Vanessa is short and stout, so she will play the role of fiancé to the play's tall and handsome hero.

This is not a good sentence because the pronoun 'she' is ambiguous. It is closer to the noun 'Vanessa', which might suggest it is Vanessa to whom 'she' is referring, but, on the other hand, a tall and handsome hero is more likely to be paired with a tall and slender fiancé, which would suggest that 'she' is Allison. But if the play that is being cast is a farce, perhaps the director wants to pair a tall and handsome hero with a short and stout heroine for additional comic effect. The point is, we cannot say for certain whom the pronoun 'she' is referring to, because of the way the sentence is constructed. This is the error known as the ambiguous pronoun reference. The writer needs to revise the sentence to clarify the ambiguous pronoun.

Allison is tall and slender so she, and not Vanessa who is short and stout, will play the role of the hero's tall and handsome fiancé.

Vanessa is short and stout, so she will play the role of the hero's tall and handsome fiancé and not Allison, who is tall and slender.

Here are five additional examples of sentences that contain ambiguous pronouns, followed by revised sentences, which clarify the relationship between the noun and pronoun. The ambiguous pronouns are underlined.

1. According to a study published in *The Journal of Psychology*, the name 'Aleisha' is associated with sex appeal, while the name 'Fiona' is associated with high social status, so the Smiths chose it as the name for their second daughter.
2. According to a study published in *The Journal of Psychology*, the name 'Aleisha' is associated with sex appeal, so the Smiths chose it as the name for their second daughter, over 'Fiona', which is associated with high social status.

According to a study published in *The Journal of Psychology*, the name 'Aleisha' is associated with sex appeal, while the name 'Fiona' is associated with high social status, so the Smiths chose Fiona as the name for their second daughter.

According to a study published in *The Journal of Psychology*, the name 'Aleisha' is associated with sex appeal, while the name 'Fiona' is associated with high social status, so the Smiths chose Aleisha as the name for their second daughter.

3. It was full of long, complex sentences and sophisticated vocabulary, which was more suitable to adult than children readers.

It was full of long, complex sentences and sophisticated vocabulary, a style which was more suitable to adult than children readers.

With its long, complex sentences and sophisticated vocabulary, its style was more suitable to adult than children readers.

4. After editing my entire collection of poetry for the seventh time, I sent three of them to the editor of *The Edinburgh Review.*

   After editing my entire collection of poetry for the seventh time, I sent three of the poems to the editor of *The Edinburgh Review.*
   After editing my entire collection of poems for the seventh time, I sent three of them to the editor of *The Edinburgh Review.*

5. In today's editorial in *The Cardiff Times,* it predicts that thousands of protesters will wear black arm band to indicate their opposition to Council's plan.

   Today's editorial in *The Cardiff Times,* predicts that thousands of protesters will wear black arm bands to indicate their opposition to Council's plan.
   The author of today's editorial in *The Cardiff Times,* predicts that thousands of protesters will wear black arm band to indicate their opposition to Council's plan.

Avoid ambiguity, as well, when you use a pronoun in a comparison. Consider these sentences:

Even Napoleon was taller than (he, him).
Arabella got the job, but she hates air travel even more than (I, me).

The terminal verb in these sentences is understood and so does not have to be written. But if you do write out that terminal verb, only to eliminate it later, your pronoun choice becomes clear:

Even Napoleon was taller than he was.
Arabella got the job, but she hates air travel even more than I do.

In some sentences that are based upon a comparison, either the subjective-case or objective-case pronoun might be acceptable, but the choice of pronoun will affect the meaning of the sentence. Consider this sentence:

> My grandfather likes Manchester United more than (I, me).

With the subjective-case pronoun 'I', the meaning of this sentence is 'My grandfather likes Manchester United more than I do'. With the objective-case 'me', the sentence means 'My grandfather likes Manchester United more than he likes me'.

Gender specific pronouns

Some pronouns signal gender. He, him, and his are, obviously, masculine; she and her are feminine. We write 'Florence Nightingale devoted <u>her</u> life to nursing'; 'John Melanton was also a liberal, but Gladstone did not like <u>him</u>'.

There are, however, scores of nouns that do not signal gender: student, teacher, manager, soldier, Prime Minister, engineer, driver, accountant, athlete, physician, professor, pharmacist—the list is a long one. Indeed, the list has grown in recent years, as some nouns that do signal gender—policeman, fireman, stewardess, waitress—have been consciously replaced by gender-neutral nouns that do not—police officer, firefighter, flight attendant, server.

When gender-neutral nouns are plural, pronouns that identify them present no problems because those pronouns—their, they, them—are gender neutral: The professors are ordering <u>their</u> regalia now. But when these nouns are singular, writers must, according to the rules of modern English usage, use both the masculine and the feminine forms of the pronoun when referencing a gender-neutral noun: Any professor who has not ordered <u>his or her</u> regalia must do so before the end of the week. There are times, however, when this need to include both pronouns can cause grammar problems. There are some rules worth knowing to help you circumvent such problems.

Rule One: Do not use a plural pronoun if its antecedent is a singular noun.

Consider this sentence:

> Any professor who has not ordered their regalia must do so before the end of the week.

This sentence contains an error in grammar, known as incorrect pronoun-antecedent agreement. An antecedent is a noun to which a pronoun refers. In the sentence above, the noun 'professor' is the antecedent of the pronoun 'their'. The error is that the word 'professor' is singular so the plural pronoun 'their' cannot be used—the pronoun does not 'agree' with its noun. The sentence should read:

> Any professor who has not ordered his or her regalia must do so before the end of the week.

or

> Professors who have not ordered their regalia must do so before the end of the week.

Here is another example.

> Each candidate will have ten minutes to present their platform.

This sentence is grammatically incorrect. 'Candidate' is singular; 'their' is plural. We can correct this sentence by making 'candidate' plural:

> Candidates will have ten minutes to present their platform.

If the writer chooses to maintain the singular—which is sometimes preferred because it can be more emphatic—then the writer must use both the masculine and the feminine form of the pronoun—Each candidate will have ten minutes to present his or her platform. Of course, if the context of the entire text had made clear that all of the candidates were, in fact, male or female, then the sentence would be correct if only one pronoun were used—Three women are running in the by-election. Each candidate will have ten minutes to present her platform.

Here is one more example:

> A student at this university will have their library privileges suspended if they accumulate more than three overdue fines.

The sentence is grammatically incorrect because 'student' is singular and 'their' is plural. The writer must make 'student' plural—Students at this university will have their library privileges suspended if they accumulate more than three overdue fines. Or the writer must include both the masculine and the feminine pronouns—A student at this university will have his or her library privileges suspended if he or she accumulates more than three overdue fines.

Rule Two: If the pronoun's antecedent is an indefinite pronoun, follow the convention of the school you are attending or the publication for which you are writing.

An indefinite pronoun is one that refers to unspecified individuals: everyone, everybody, nobody, anyone, all, anybody. Indefinite pronouns are, as a rule, singular: Everyone is (not are) happy; nobody is (not are) sad. Although these sentences clearly indicate that indefinite pronouns are usually singular, writers often use a plural pronoun following an indefinite pronoun to which the plural pronoun is referring. Consider this sentence:

> Anyone who has not ordered their regalia must do so by the end of the week.

The indefinite pronoun 'anyone' is clearly singular, followed as it is by the verb 'has' not 'have'. Yet the plural pronoun 'their' is used later in the sentence to refer to 'anyone'. Strictly speaking, this is an error in grammar: lack of agreement in number. Strictly speaking, a singular pronoun should follow 'anyone'. Actually, two singular pronouns should follow 'anyone' because 'anyone' is gender neutral.

> Anyone who has not ordered his or her regalia must do so by the end of the week.

Here are two more examples:

> No one will be ruled out unless they have committed a crime.
> Everyone drove their own car, even though it was a meeting of environmentalists.

Strictly speaking, these sentences should be revised as follows:

> No one will be ruled out unless he or she has committed a crime.
> Everyone drove his or her own car, even though it was a meeting of environmentalists.

However, the use of the plural pronouns 'they', 'them', and 'their' in reference to an indefinite pronoun is becoming so widespread that many teachers, professors, and editors overlook the error. The use of the plural pronoun has practically become standard with relative pronouns such as 'who', even though these pronouns are singular: Who is (not are) present? But this usage—Who doesn't love their children?—is probably more common than this—Who doesn't love his or her children?

What should you do? Check with the teacher, professor, or editor who is going to judge your writing. Find out what his or her policy is on the use of plural pronouns in reference to indefinite pronouns and follow that policy.

A digression: *Fowler's Modern English Usage*

In the 1920s, a retired school teacher named Henry Fowler wrote the *Dictionary of Modern English Usage,* which was published in 1926. It became a bestseller and the acknowledged authority on English usage. Educated people kept it close by, consulted it when they needed an answer to a grammar or usage question, referenced it when they chided others for committing an error in grammar or usage. 'Why must you write *intensive* here?' Winston Churchill wrote to the Director of Military Intelligence, as the Director was planning the invasion of Normandy. '*Intense* is the right word. You should read Fowler's *Modern English Usage* on the use of the two words'.

In the mid-1990s, the distinguished lexicographer Robert Burchfield revised and updated the book, ensuring that it would continue to be the acknowledged authority on English usage. The author of every book about grammar and usage, including the author of *Perfect Grammar*, owes a debt to Henry Fowler.

What does *The New Fowler's Modern English Usage* have to say about the use of the plural pronoun in reference to an indefinite pronoun? Burchfield cites numerous examples of its widespread use, including:

> Everybody does and says what <u>they</u> please.
> Everyone was absorbed in <u>their</u> own business.
> I resent it when I call someone who is not home, and <u>they</u> don't have an answering machine.

He concludes that 'This is the way the language naturally operates, despite the obvious clash of number between the pronoun and what follows' (p. 270). This 'violation of grammatical concord', he continues, is sometimes necessary (p. 271).

Rule Three: Revise a sentence that repeats both the masculine and feminine pronoun ad nauseum

The need to include both the masculine and the feminine pronoun when its antecedent is a gender-neutral noun can adversely affect the rhythm of a sentence if the pronouns have to be repeated too frequently. Consider this sentence:

> A Member of Parliament should communicate with his or her constituents on a regular basis, letting

> them know, especially, what his or her position on the important issues of the day is, and how he or she will vote on each bill as it is presented in the House.

One repetition of both the masculine and feminine pronoun is fine, two is not highly desirable but is tolerable, three is too much—the rhythm and flow of the sentence is interrupted, as the above sentence illustrates. Revise such sentences to avoid this jarring rhythm.

One possible revision for the above sentence is to eliminate the first 'his or her'. The revision may be less exact, but it will be more graceful. Another possibility is to pluralise the noun because then the gender neutral 'they', 'them', or 'their' can be substituted.

> Members of Parliament should communicate with their constituents on a regular basis, letting them know, especially, what their position on the important issues of the day is, and how they will vote on each bill as it is presented in the House.

'Constituents' is also plural, of course, so some clarity may be lost in the maze of plural pronouns, but, again, the gain in fluidity may trump a minor loss in clarity.

Here is another example:

> When a soldier is given a command that he or she feels he or she cannot obey, he or she may ask that the command be issued in writing.

Most readers will agree that the repetition of both the masculine and the feminine pronouns impairs this sentence's rhythm. A switch to the plural results in a sentence that loses some emphasis but is still better than the original:

> When soldiers are given commands that they feel they cannot obey, they may ask that the command be issued in writing.

Other solutions to this problem of excessive repetition have been suggested. Some grammarians, noting that for hundreds of years the exclusive use of the masculine was standard, argue that, to redress the historical imbalance, the feminine pronoun form should be used exclusively now, and some academic journals have taken this argument to heart and do privilege the feminine form. Other grammarians argue that the language needs a gender neutral singular pronoun and have suggested we welcome new pronouns such as 'te', 'tis', and 'ter' into the language. This suggestion has not caught on.

It is also important that commonsense prevail when you are making rhetorical decisions that involve gender. Some nouns may be gender neutral but have gender specific connotations—synchronised swimmer, linebacker, gangster, dressmaker, tailor—and most readers would not object to the use of a gender-specific singular pronoun in reference to such nouns. It may be best, though, to err on the side of caution. Not that long ago nouns like 'boxer' and 'prize fighter' had strong masculine connotations, but in an era when a movie about a female boxer wins several academy awards (*Million Dollar Baby*), such connotations evolve.

Tutorial

Progress questions

Revise the following sentences to correct any errors you detect in the use of pronouns.

1. If a magician has long fingers, their sleight-of-hand tricks are more impressive.
2. Each student who applies for admission to the Certified Mid-wife Program must show proof that she has a degree or certificate in nursing.
3. The Arsenal midfielder claimed he was only joking, but even many of his own teammates didn't appreciate it.
4. If a client does not lose at least ten pounds within the first month, they will get a full refund.
5. The stylist braided the bride's hair, then festooned each one with a pink ribbon.
6. In 2003, illusionist David Blaine, lived in a Plexiglas pod near Tower Bridge for 44 days, but most Londoners did not appreciate it.
7. In Evelyn Waugh's *Brideshead Revisited*, he portrays the decline of a prominent Roman Catholic family.
8. A parent who wants to make sure their child has a head start when they attend school will read to them every day.
9. In *Wikipedia* it says that Edgar Allen Poe spent time in Philadelphia.
10. An Anglican bishop must visit the parishes for which they are responsible regularly.

Define and provide, in a sentence, an example of the following terms:

1. pronoun
2. antecedent
3. lack of agreement in number
4. lack of agreement in gender
5. indefinite pronoun.

Discussion point

Do you agree that both the masculine and feminine forms of the pronoun should be used when their antecedent is a singular gender-neutral noun? Do you agree that gender-specific suffixes such as 'man' (policeman) and 'ess' (actress) should be expunged from the language?

Practical assignment

Explore online magazine articles written in the 1950s, and see if you can detect examples of what we might consider today to be sexist language.

Study and revision tip

Remember to revise any sentences you have written that repeat the masculine and feminine forms of the pronoun more than twice.

Answers to the progress questions

Revise the following sentences to correct any errors you detect in the use of pronouns.

1. If a magician has long fingers, <u>his or her</u> sleight-of-hand tricks are more impressive.
2. Each student who applies for admission to the Certified Mid-Wife Program must show proof that he or she has a degree or certificate in nursing.
3. The Arsenal midfielder claimed he was only joking, but even many of his own teammates didn't appreciate <u>the joke</u>.
4. If a client does not lose at least ten pounds within the first month, <u>he or she</u> will get a full refund.
5. The stylist braided the bride's hair, then festooned each <u>braid</u> with a pink ribbon.
6. In 2003, illusionist David Blaine, lived in a Plexiglas pod near Tower Bridge for 44 days, but most Londoners did not appreciate <u>the stunt</u>.
7. In *Brideshead Revisited*, Evelyn Waugh portrays the decline of a prominent Catholic family.
8. <u>Parents</u> who want to make sure their child has a head start when they attend school will read to them every day.
9. *Wikipedia* <u>states</u> that Edgar Allen Poe spent time in Philadelphia.

10. An Anglican Bishop must visit the parishes for which he or she is responsible regularly.

Define and provide, in a sentence, an example of the following terms.

1. pronoun: a word that takes the place of a noun.
2. antecedent: the noun to which a pronoun that follows and identifies that noun refers.
3. lack of agreement in number: error that occurs when a pronoun is plural but its antecedent is singular—A person should see their dentist twice a year.
4. lack of agreement in gender: the use of just one gender-specific pronoun when both are needed—A surgeon must wash his hands often.
5. indefinite pronoun: a pronoun that refers to an unidentified noun—anyone, somebody, everyone.

6 Pronoun case

One-minute summary

Pronouns are those short words such as he, she, I, me, you, they, that take the place of a noun. There are many pronouns in the English language, and they are divided into three types or <u>cases</u>: subjective, objective, and possessive. Errors in pronoun case are common, and writers must exercise care in selecting pronouns in the correct case. In this Chapter, pronoun case is defined and described and the rules you need to know to avoid common errors in pronoun case are presented. These rules are:

- Select the correct pronoun when a pronoun is paired with a noun.
- Use 'who' and 'whom' in their appropriate context.
- Use possessive case before a gerund, objective case before a participle.
- Use the subjective case after the verb 'to be'.
- Avoid misusing the reflexive pronoun.

Definition

Pronouns come in three forms or cases, subjective, objective, and possessive. A subject-case pronoun is used as the subject of a verb (<u>She</u> cried); an object-case pronoun is used as the object of a verb (I like <u>her</u>) or a preposition (I am with <u>her</u>); a possessive-case pronoun is used to indicate ownership (It's <u>his</u> pen). Here is a pronoun chart, arranged by case.

When we are writing, we usually select the pronoun that sounds the best in the context in which it occurs, and we are usually correct, especially if our native tongue is English. It is unlikely that we would select the wrong pronoun in our simple sample sentences above—Her cried; I like she; I am

Subjective Case	Objective Case	Possessive Case
I	Me	My
We	Us	Our
She	Her	His
He	Him	Her
They	Them	Their
You	You	Your(s)
Who	Whom	Whose
It	It	Its

with he; It is him pen—not because we consciously think that a subject, object, or possessive-case pronoun is correct in this context, but because we know what 'sounds right'. More often than not, our ear will not let us down.

There are times, however, when pronoun case can trip us up, and it is at times like these when we have to know the rules.

Select the proper case when the pronoun is paired with a noun

From an early age, we are taught to use the subjective case of the pronoun when that pronoun is paired with a noun: My father and <u>I</u> both went to Cambridge, never My father and me went to Cambridge or Me and my father went to Cambridge. But when the pronoun is paired with a noun that is the object of a verb or a preposition, the pronoun must switch to the objective case. Note that without that noun, we select the objective case naturally, as a matter of course:

Cambridge taught <u>me</u> how to think for myself.

But because we learned so well to use the subjective case of the pronoun when the pronoun is paired with a noun acting as a subject, that combination became automatic, it always sounded right, and so we continued to use the subjective case pronoun even when it was paired with a noun acting as an object.

> Cambridge taught my father and I to think for ourselves.

But this sentence is grammatically incorrect. Remove the noun, and the error becomes obvious:

> Cambridge taught I to think for myself.

In this sentence, the pronoun is the object of the verb 'taught', and it must be in objective case, whether or not it is paired with a noun. This is the grammatically correct version:

> Cambridge taught my father and me to think for ourselves.

The same rule applies when a pronoun is paired with a noun acting as the object of a preposition. We know this sentence is grammatically incorrect:

> Oxford was the right university for I to attend.

It sounds all wrong. The subjective 'I' must be changed to the objective 'me' because of the preposition 'for'. The sentence is still wrong, if we pair the pronoun with a noun:

> Oxford was the right university for my mother and I to attend.

Whether alone or paired with a noun, a pronoun must be in objective case, if it is the object of a preposition:

> Oxford was the right university for me to attend.
> Oxford was the right university for my mother and me to attend.

Here are five more examples of sentences that are grammatically incorrect because the writer has paired the wrong pronoun with a noun.

1. Certainly us and maybe even American car buyers will be dazzled by the design of the new Jaguar XK.

This sentence has two subjects 'us' and 'the Americans'. Delete the second subject and it becomes clear that the pronoun 'us' is not in the correct case.

Us will be dazzled by the design of the new Jaguar XK.

'Us' is an objective-case pronoun, used when its subjective case counterpart 'we' is required:

We will be dazzled ... Certainly we and maybe even American car buyers will be dazzled by the design of the new Jaguar XK.

If we turn the sentence around, then the objective case 'us' would be correct because it would be the object, not the subject of the verb 'will dazzle':

The design of the new Jaguar XK will dazzle <u>us</u> and maybe even American car buyers.

2. Jaguar's chief of automotive design and him will work together to create a car that will rival the sleek design of the Mercedes-Benz CLS.

This sentence has two subjects 'chief' and 'him'. But 'him' is an objective-case pronoun, so it cannot be used as a subject. We cannot write 'Him will work'. The subjective case 'he' must be used:

Jaguar's chief of automotive design and <u>he</u> will work together to create a car that will rival the sleek design of the Mercedes-Benz CLS.

3. Our marketing manager will work with the chief of automotive design and she to create a car that will rival the sleek design of the Mercedes-Benz CLS.

Now we have the subjective-case pronoun 'she' doing work its objective-case counterpart 'her' is supposed to be doing. The objective case is used after a preposition, such as 'with'. Our marketing manager will work with 'her', hence:

Our marketing manager will work with the chief of automotive design and <u>her</u> to create a car that will rival the sleek design of the Mercedes-Benz CLS.

4. If auto makers ever design a functional car for my family and I, they would sacrifice an elegant, in favour of practical design that would cost less.

In this sentence, delete the noun 'family' that accompanies the pronoun 'I' and it becomes obvious that 'I's' objective-case counterpart 'me' is the correct choice to make: design a car for me, hence:

> If auto makers ever design a functional car for my family and <u>me</u>, they would sacrifice an elegant, in favour of practical design that would cost less.

5. After the demonstration, the professional driver gave they and the company president a ride up the winding roads of Bear Mountain to demonstrate the car's superior handling.

In this sentence the pronoun 'they' is used incorrectly because it follows the verb 'gave', which, like almost all verbs, should be followed by an objective-case pronoun. He gave <u>them</u> not they a ride, hence:

> After the demonstration, the professional driver gave <u>them</u> and the company president a ride up the winding roads of Bear Mountain to demonstrate the car's superior handling.

Avoid misuse of who and whom

'Who' is a subjective-case pronoun, while 'whom' is its objective-case counterpart. Usually, we will select the correct pronoun for the rhetorical context within which it is to be used because we know what 'sounds right'. 'Never send to know <u>for whom</u> the bell tolls', wrote John Donne, correctly using the objective case after the preposition, 'it tolls for thee'. <u>To Whom It May Concern</u> we write, correctly using the objective case after the preposition, when we are uncertain of the identity of our letter or email's recipient. Similarly, we write <u>Who</u> else knows about this? <u>Who</u> cares? <u>Who</u> writes letters any more? because we know the verbs (knows, cares, writes) require subjects and that the objective form of the pronoun—Whom cares?—would be bizarre.

Confusion often arises, however, when the need for an object or a subject is not so readily apparent. Consider this sentence:

> The congregation does not know (who or whom) Father Doyle will hire as the new bell-ringer.

Our choice here seems more difficult because more is going on in the sentence. There are two subject-verb combinations: The congregation does not know; and Father Doyle will hire. The best way to determine which pronoun is the correct one is to isolate the clause within which who or whom is to appear. In this sentence that clause is, obviously, Father Doyle will hire. Now the verb for this clause is 'will hire'; and who is doing the hiring, who, in other words, is the subject of the clause. Clearly that subject is 'Father Doyle'. If, then, we already have a subject for the clause, it is the object that is missing. 'Whom', therefore, is the correct pronoun for this sentence:

> The congregation does not know whom Father Doyle will hire as the new bell-ringer.

Now consider this sentence:

> Sister Francis is the only member of the committee (who, whom) the bell-ringer knows is going to support his application for more funding.

Ignore, again, for the moment, the sentence's first clause, which will not influence the pronoun selection. Concentrate on the second clause. Now this clause has a subject and a verb—'the bell-ringer knows'—which might make us think the objective case is required. But wait: there is another verb here—'is going'. This verb needs a subject. We would not write 'Whom is going'. Here, 'who' is the right choice. A verb needs its subject:

> Sister Francis is the only member of the committee who the bell-ringer knows is going to support his application for more funding.

There are similar challenges when a sentence calls for the use of who or whom with a preposition. For whom the bell tolls and to whom it may concern are well-known preposition-whom combinations and do not make trouble. But if the preposition is stranded at the end of a sentence—we don't know (who, whom) the bell is tolling for—the objective *whom* often loses out to its subjective partner *who*, even though *whom* is still the preposition's object and should be used. The Digression Box in Chapter One warns against ending a sentence with a preposition and uses this sentence as an example: It was my first day of work, and I did not even know who I was supposed to report to. Again, in this sentence the 'who' should be a 'whom' even though it has almost lost its preposition. It is especially unwise, then, to end a sentence with a preposition, when the pronoun that accompanies it is 'whom'.

Now there are times when times when 'who' and not 'whom' will follow a preposition. Recall from Chapter One that a noun clause can function as an object, either of a verb—I know whom you love the most—or of a preposition—I know for whom the bell tolls. But if the clause that follows the preposition does not contain a subject, then the pronoun 'who' will function as the subject. In the sentence 'I know for whom the bell tolls' bell is the subject of the noun clause and tolls is its verb. But consider these sentences:

The computer is there for whoever needs it.
Give these earplugs to whoever is tolling the bell.

We see the preposition 'for' in the first sentence and the preposition 'to' in the second sentence and our instinct might tell us to follow it with the objective case of the pronoun—'whom'—and not the subjective—'who'. But a clause's verb needs a subject. In the noun clause in the first sentence, the verb 'needs' requires a subject, which is why the subjective case of the pronoun is used. The entire clause 'whoever needs it' is the object of the preposition 'for'. The same holds true for the second sentence. The verb 'is tolling' needs the subjective 'whoever' and the entire clause 'whoever is tolling the bell' is the object of the preposition 'to'.

Use possessive case before a gerund, objective case before a participle

A gerund is a word that is derived from a verb but functions in a sentence as a noun. 'To drive' for example is a verb: We are driving to Liverpool tomorrow. But if we use 'driving' as the subject or object of a sentence, 'driving' is functioning not as a verb but as a noun and is called a gerund. A gerund always ends in 'ing'. Driving is fun; I like driving.

If you use a pronoun before a gerund, the pronoun should be in possessive case. Consider these sentences:

> Parents are getting increasingly uneasy about their children's access to the Internet but the new software will make <u>their monitoring</u> the content of certain websites much easier.
>
> The committee objected to <u>his monitoring</u> the content of every website employees accessed.
>
> <u>Their dancing</u> was perfect.

In the first sentence, 'monitoring' is the object of the verb 'will make', so it acts as a gerund, and is, therefore, preceded by the possessive case—their—of the pronoun. In the second sentence, 'monitoring' is the object of the preposition 'to', so it acts as a gerund and is, therefore, preceded by the possessive case—his—of the pronoun. In the third sentence, 'dancing' is the subject of the verb 'was', so it functions as a gerund and is, therefore, preceded by the possessive case—their—of the pronoun.

Now it is important to distinguish between a gerund and a present participle. A present participle is also derived from a verb and also ends in 'ing', so it looks exactly like a gerund. The difference is that a present participle functions not as a noun but as an adjective. In this sentence—They installed a new operating system—'operating' is a present participle, but, in this sentence—Operating the new system is not difficult—'operating' is a gerund. Similarly, in this sentence—We decided starting over was our best option—'starting' is a gerund, while in this sentence—We knew from the starting point, the new software would cause problems—'starting' is a participle. If a pronoun is called for before a participle, the objective case of the pronoun is required. Consider these sentences:

We saw him driving another new car.
Her father did not want to see them dancing too closely.

In the first sentence, 'driving' is a participle because it is derived from a verb (to drive), but it is functioning as an adjective. It is preceded, therefore, by the objective case (him) and not the possessive (his), as it would be if it were functioning as a noun. Similarly, in the second sentence, 'dancing' is adjectival, so it is preceded by the objective case (them) of the pronoun.

Often, either the objective or the possessive case is acceptable before an 'ing' word, but the choice effects the meaning of the sentence. Consider these sentences:

The jury did not appreciate <u>him</u> intimidating the witness.
The jury did not appreciate <u>his</u> intimidating the witness.

Both sentences are grammatically correct, but they differ subtly in meaning. In the first sentence, the stress is on 'him'; in the second, it is on the 'intimidating'. This is because in the first sentence 'him' is the object of the verb 'did not appreciate', while, in the second sentence, the gerund 'intimidating' is the verb's object.

Use the subjective case after the verb 'to be'

Earlier in this Chapter, you learned that the objective case of the pronoun is regularly used after a verb: We write I know him, not I know he. But there is an exception to this usage. Following a form of the verb 'to be', when that verb is used as the main verb of a sentence, and when that verb is followed by a pronoun, you should use the subjective, not the objective case of the pronoun. This rule seems anomalous, but, really, it is not. Consider these two sentences:

Beckham knows the Captain.
Beckham is the Captain.

In the first sentence, Beckham and the Captain are two different people, but in the second sentence Beckham and the Captain are the same people. The verb 'is', a form of the verb 'to be', establishes that relationship. Because of this, 'Captain' is another form of the sentence's subject 'Beckham', and this is why, if we changed 'Captain' in the second sentence to a pronoun, that pronoun would be the subjective 'he'. In the first sentence, the pronoun would be 'him'. So:

Beckham knows him.
Beckham is he.

'He' may not sound right because we are so used to hearing the objective case after a verb, but it is the grammatically correct pronoun to use in this sentence. Here are some other examples:

It was <u>she</u> who was misinformed.
The only person in my family interested in philosophy is <u>I</u>.

A digression: On condoning errors in English grammar

As the subjective-case-after-the-verb-to be-rule suggests, there are some rules of English grammar that can create sentences that are correct but sound incorrect. Consider this sentence:

The children were blamed for the vandalism, but the real culprits are they.

Most English speakers would say 'them', not 'they', at the end of this sentence, and many would write 'them' as well. Most readers who saw 'them' at the end of this sentence would not shake their heads in dismay and think to themselves, 'yet another error in grammar'. Some would argue that we should condone certain errors in grammar, especially those that are committed so frequently in speech and in writing that they no longer seem to be errors. Others would counter, noting that the rule is not arbitrary. There is a good reason why 'they' and not 'them' belongs at the end of the sentence: it refers to 'culprits', a word which is clearly a subjective. There is a way out of such dilemmas. You always have the option of recasting a sentence in order to avoid a usage that sounds stilted, even if it is correct:

The children were blamed for the vandalism, but they are the real culprits. They are the real culprits, even though the children were blamed for the vandalism.

Avoid misuse of the reflexive pronoun

Reflexive pronouns are those that refer back to a 'self' identified earlier in the sentence: myself, himself, herself, themselves, ourselves. Here are some examples:

Eric refused to go by himself.
I can't do it all myself.
They have only themselves to blame.

The reflexive pronouns are used correctly in these sentences because they refer to an earlier noun or pronoun which cannot be replaced meaningfully with a regular-case pronoun. The meaning of the sentence changes entirely, for example, if we do use a regular-case pronoun—Eric refused to go by him. But you should avoid using a reflexive pronoun, if you can replace it meaningfully with either the regular objective or subjective case form. Consider these sentences:

The officers were responsible, but the sergeant and myself were under suspicion.
She plans to take legal action because there are, on the disk, some intimate scenes between Stella and myself.

In the first sentence, 'myself' is, with 'sergeant' the subject of the verb 'were' and, therefore, should be replaced with the subjective case—I—of the pronoun. In the second sentence, 'myself' is, with 'Stella', the object of the preposition 'between' and, therefore, should be replaced with the objective case—me—of the pronoun.

Tutorial

Progress questions

Revise the following sentences to correct any errors you detect in the use of pronouns.

1. Ellis's guardian left a fortune to his step-brother, whom I believe now lives in Mexico.
2. The table was carefully set for my bridegroom and I.
3. Making the 500-mile journey in covered wagons, they learned to fend for theirselves.
4. The controversial politician and him were to meet to try to work out a settlement.
5. It was her who insisted the meeting take place at the Savoy.
6. Desperate, they turned the case over to a firm of lawyers who they felt they could trust.
7. My wife is more tolerant of celebrities who express political opinions than me.
8. In quick succession, the audience booed Casey, then Kean, then I off the stage.
9. After the jury learned of him torturing even small children, the outcome of the trial was no longer in doubt.
10. No one can impersonate the bishop like him.
11. The outcome of the election was not good news for we conservatives.

Define and provide, in a sentence, an example of the following terms:

1. Reflexive pronoun
2. Subjective-case pronoun
3. Objective-case pronoun
4. Possessive-case pronoun
5. Gerund
6. Present participle.

Discussion point

Discuss the implications of this Chapters 'Digression: On Condoning Errors in English Grammar'.

Practical assignment

Make a list, in what you consider to be the descending order of frequency, of common pronoun-case errors.

Study and revision tip

Some errors in pronoun case will go unnoticed by recipients of casual emails and other informal forms of writing. But if you are writing for publication or for a school grade, double check your drafts to make certain you have made no errors in pronoun case.

Answers to the progress questions

Revise the following sentences to correct any errors you detect in the case of the pronouns.

1. Ellis's guardian left a fortune to Ellis's step-brother, who I believe now lives in Mexico.
2. The table was carefully set for my bridegroom and [for] me.
3. Making the 500-mile journey in covered wagons, they learned to fend for themselves.
4. The controversial politician and he were to meet to try to work out a settlement.
5. It was she who insisted the meeting take place at the Savoy.
6. Desperate, they turned the case over to a firm of lawyers whom they felt they could trust.
7. My wife is more tolerant of celebrities who express political opinions than I [am].
8. In quick succession, the audience booed Casey, then Kean, then me off the stage.
9. After the jury learned of his torturing even small children, the outcome of the trial was no longer in doubt.
10. No one can impersonate the bishop like he [can].
11. The outcome of the election was not good news for us conservatives.

Define and provide, in a sentence, an example of the following terms.

1. reflexive pronoun: a pronoun with 'self' as its suffix: himself, herself, myself, themselves.
2. antecedent: the noun to which a pronoun that follows and identifies that noun refers. John forgot his lunch.
3. lack of agreement in number: error that occurs when a pronoun is plural but its antecedent is singular: A person should see their dentist twice a year.
4. lack of agreement in gender: the use of just one gender-specific pronoun when both are needed—A surgeon must wash his hands thoroughly before operating.
5. indefinite pronoun: a pronoun that refers to an unidentified noun—anyone, somebody, everyone.

7 Subject-verb agreement

One-minute summary

In Chapter One, we learned that the essence of an English sentence is a subject and a verb, a noun doing something: The sun rises; birds sing; children play; we work; the whistle blows; evening comes; time flies. The sentence's subject and verb must agree. If the subject is singular, the verb must be singular; if the subject is plural, the verb must be plural. We could not write 'birds sings' because 'birds' is the plural form of the noun and 'sings' is the singular form of the verb. (It is an eccentricity of the English language that the addition of an 's' often makes a noun plural but a verb, singular). We could not write 'a bird sing' because 'bird' is the singular form of the noun and 'sing' is the plural form of the verb.

Unfortunately, subject-verb agreement is not always this simple and direct. You might need to pause and remember the grammar rule that prescribes proper agreement if:

- words come between your subject and verb;
- you use a collective noun;
- your sentence uses more than one subject;
- your subject is an indefinite pronoun; or
- your subject is followed by a plural complement.

The purpose of this Chapter is to explain these rules to you.

Beware of words that come between a subject and its verb

A verb agrees with its subject, which is often the noun or pronoun that precedes it: The cost is high; the ties are expensive. But when other words intervene between the subject and the verb, less experienced writers may agree the verb with one of those words instead of with the subject. Which of these sentences is correct? Which one contains an error in subject-verb agreement?

The cost of the ties depend upon the quality of the fabric.
The cost of the ties depends upon the quality of the fabric.

The subject of this sentence is 'cost', not 'ties', despite the fact that 'ties' is closer to the verb 'depends'. Therefore, the second sentence is correct because it is the one that agrees the verb 'depends' with the subject 'cost'. The word 'ties' is the object of the preposition 'of'. Mistaking an object of a preposition for the subject of the sentence is an error less experienced writers frequently make. Be careful to agree your verbs with their true subjects.

Here are three more sentences that contain errors in subject-verb agreement, because the verb agrees not with its subject but with a word that comes between the subject and the verb. Each sentence is followed by an explanation of the error.

If even one of the numbers are wrong, the account will be closed.
The subject of the introductory clause is 'one' not 'numbers'. One is singular so the singular verb 'is' must be used.

The report issued by the Senate Committee on Reparations have to be tabled until the next session of Congress.
The subject of the sentence is the singular 'report' not the plural 'reparations' so the plural verb 'have' must be changed to the singular verb 'has'.

The Chief Executive Officer of the Omega group of companies visit the plant in Exeter at least twice a year.
The subject of the sentence is the singular 'officer' not the plural 'companies' so the plural verb 'visit' must be changed to the singular verb 'visits'.

The collective noun

A collective noun is a word that identifies a group, usually of individuals. Team, press, group, band, government, faculty, union, committee, staff—there are scores of collective nouns. In British English, the collective noun may take either a singular verb or a plural verb, though there are some collective nouns that form such a tight knit unit that the plural verb sounds discordant. Study these sentences:

> The press is demanding a news conference. The press are demanding a news conference.
> The finance committee meets every Tuesday. The finance committee meet every Tuesday.
> No other orchestra plays Mahler with so much passion. [But not No other orchestra play Mahler with so much passion].

In American English, the convention is to use the singular verb. But if the subject is followed by a prepositional phrase, beginning usually with 'of', then the object of 'of' might influence agreement and urge the writer, correctly, to use the plural. Here are some examples:

> A jubilation of larks sing outside my bedroom every morning.
> One group of tourists are ill and will stay aboard ship this morning.
> Our band of brothers are determined to fight until we achieve victory.

Sentences with more than one subject

Sentences often contain more than one subject: Jack and Jill went up the hill. If the two subjects are separated by the coordinate conjunction 'and', the verb is plural. If they are separated by the coordinate conjunction 'or' (or 'nor'), the verb agrees with the subject closest to it. Study these sentences:

The subject and the object of a sentence <u>are</u> usually nouns or pronouns.
A jacket and tie <u>are</u> required.
Ballroom dancing or roller hockey <u>is</u> to become the newest Olympic sport.
One apple or two oranges <u>provide</u> a fourth of the recommended daily amount of fiber.
Two apples or one orange <u>provides</u> a fourth of the recommended daily amount of vitamin C.
Neither my sister nor my brothers <u>are</u> mentioned in the will.
Neither my brothers nor my sister <u>is</u> mentioned in the will.

Note, especially, that sentences that join subjects together with 'or' or 'nor' agree their verb with the closest subject: oranges provide; orange provides; brothers are; sister is.

Prepositional and other phrases that are synonymous with 'and' do not affect subject-verb agreement. Such phrases include 'along with', 'together with', 'accompanied by', 'as well as', and 'not to mention'. If the subject that precedes such phrases is singular the verb is singular; if the subject is plural the verb is plural. Study these sentences:

The family's youngest daughter, along with her mother, father, brother, and grandfather, <u>is</u> travelling to Florida to compete in a beauty pageant.
The family's two daughters, together with their brother, <u>are</u> travelling to Florida to compete in a beauty pageant.
The Tio Corporation, not to mentions the many other firms that manufacture fine furniture, <u>is</u> refusing to purchase mahogany from Indonesia.

The first sentence has a singular subject 'daughter' so its verb 'is travelling' is also singular, even though other family members are also travelling. In the second sentence the subject 'daughters' is plural so the verb also becomes plural even though the singular 'brother' intervenes. In the third sentence, the singular verb 'is refusing' agrees with the singular noun 'Corporation' and not with the plural 'firms' in the 'not to mention' phrase.

Agreement and the indefinite pronoun

Indefinite pronouns identify anonymous nouns: everyone, neither, anyone, all, no one, none, everybody, somebody. The agreement rule for indefinite pronouns asserts that indefinite pronouns take singular verbs. Consider these sentences:

Everyone is here so the meeting may begin.
If anyone wants honey, it is on the top shelf.
All of the money is missing.
Somebody always shovels the snow from my sidewalk.
Neither one of my math teachers is well qualified.

In some sentences, however, a noun intervening between the indefinite pronoun and the verb is so dominant that it may overpower the indefinite pronoun and influence agreement. Strictly speaking, we should write 'None of the bills has been made into law' and not 'None of the bills have been made into law'. But the latter usage is acceptable based upon what the *New Fowler's* (see page 35) deems to be 'contextual considerations'.

You will recall, from Chapter 5, that the rule that governs pronoun agreement with an indefinite pronoun is equally malleable. Strictly speaking, we should write 'If anyone wants honey, he or she will have to bring his or her own'. But the plural pronoun is widely used, even in prestigious publications, especially now when the quest for gender equality in language is an issue. The sentence, then, could be correctly written as 'If anyone wants honey, they will have to bring their own'. Few teachers or editors will still accept the sole use of the masculine pronoun in such sentences.

A digression: The exception to the rule

English grammar is infamous for its rules that come with exceptions. In this Chapter, for example, you have learned that a subject must agree with its verb and not with words that intervene between the subject and the verb. But consider these two sentences:

All of the money is missing.

All of the students are present.

In both sentences the subject is 'all' but the verb is singular in the first sentence and plural in the second. An exception to the rule: In some sentences the verb will agree with the object of a preposition, not the subject of the sentence.

Similarly, you learned that plural subjects take singular verbs. But some subjects are plural in form—news, physics, Keeblers—but singular in meaning and, therefore, take singular verbs: The news is on Channel 11. Physics is a fascinating subject. Keeblers is marketing a new potato crisp flavour. *Star Wars* is on Channel 4 tonight. An exception to the rule: some subjects are plural but take a singular noun because their connotation is singular.

Recall, as well, the exceptions to the rules we have covered in other Chapters. Sentence fragments (Chapter Two) are usually unacceptable but are fine when they are used deliberately for emphasis. Indefinite pronouns (Chapter 5) are singular so nouns and pronouns that are their antecedents must also be singular, but there are times when the plural is acceptable. Despite the error, this sentence: Who has their children with them? is better than this sentence: Who has his or her children with him or her? The subjective case of the pronoun is supposed to follow the verb 'to be' (Chapter 6), but certain objective pronouns are so commonly used, their inappropriateness goes unnoticed and they have become acceptable, even preferable. Most editors would prefer 'That's him in the front row' to 'That's he's in the front row', even if the 'he' obeys a rule.

Singular verbs with plural complements

Recall from Chapter 6 that linking verbs—the most common of which is the verb 'to be'—take complements, not objects. If you write a sentence with a plural subject followed by a form of the verb 'to be' followed by a singular complement, you will usually use a plural verb automatically and correctly:

> In Aruba, wild parties <u>were</u> an everyday event.
> The palace and its lush garden <u>were</u> a magnet for tourists.

However, if you write a sentence with a singular subject followed by a form of the verb 'to be' followed by a plural complement, you need to be careful to use the singular form of the verb because the plural might sound better. Study these sentences carefully:

> In Aruba, an everyday event <u>was</u> wild parties going on at all hours all over the island.
> The problem <u>was</u> the lush gardens which were getting too expensive to maintain.
> The only issue <u>is</u> the rights of the child.

Tutorial

Progress questions

Correct subject-verb agreement errors in these sentences.

1. The pawnbroker could not say if his pens or his watch were worth more money.
2. His pen and his watch is made by the same company and is very expensive.
3. A guitar with twelve strings have a better sound than one with six.
4. The indecision among the judges are going to delay the verdict.
5. His first but not his second wife are invited.
6. *Great Expectations* are my favourite Dickens' novel.
7. Watching a movie or reading a book are a good way for children to pass time on a long road trip.
8. His luggage and his laptop has gone missing, even though it was a brief flight from London to Liverpool.
9. One of the dancers have a prosthetic leg.
10. Someone from the Royal Family, probably either the prince or the princess, have promised to attend.

Define each of the following terms:

1. Subject-verb agreement
2. Collective noun
3. Indefinite pronoun
4. Subject complement
5. Prepositional phrase.

Discussion point

Consider the similarities and differences between pronoun-antecedent agreement and subject-verb agreement.

Practical assignment

Make a list of the three subject-verb agreement errors that you believe you are most likely to make in your writing. For each error, write a sentence that illustrates the error followed by a revised and corrected sentence.

Study and revision tip

Consult the entry for 'Agree' in *The New Fowler's Modern English Usage* for additional information on both subject-verb and pronoun-antecedent agreement.

Answers to the progress questions

Correct subject-verb agreement errors in these sentences.

1. The pawnbroker could not say if his pens or his watch was worth more money.
2. His pen and his watch are made by the same company and are very expensive.
3. A guitar with twelve strings has a better sound than one with six.
4. The indecision among the judges is going to delay the verdict.
5. His first but not his second wife is invited.
6. *Great Expectations* is my favourite Dickens' novel.
7. Watching a movie or reading a book is a good way for children to pass time on a long road trip.
8. His luggage and his laptop have gone missing, even though it was a brief flight from London to Liverpool.
9. One of the dancers has a prosthetic leg.
10. Someone from the Royal Family, probably either the prince or the princess, has promised to attend.

Define each of the following terms

Subject-verb agreement: a principle of grammar asserting that the number of the subject determines the number of the verb; singular verbs have singular subjects; plural verbs take plural subjects.

Collective noun: one that identifies a grouping such as team, family, choir; usually followed by a singular verb: my family is crazy.

Indefinite pronoun: one that identifies a homogenous but amorphous group such as everyone, all, someone; usually take a singular verb but may take a plural pronoun: Everyone has their own reasons.

Subject complement: noun, pronoun, or adjective that follows form of verb 'to be' and that identifies, qualifies, or complements the subject: Eric is sad; Henry is the captain.

Prepositional phrase: a group of words that begins with a preposition and ends with a noun or pronoun called the object of the preposition: in the army.

8 Verb tense

One-minute summary

A verb is that part of speech that expresses action. An action can occur separately or within a context that includes other actions. A verb must have enough forms to express clearly, especially those actions that occur in the context of others. English verbs do have many forms, and writers must be careful to select the form that expresses most clearly and correctly the nature of the action expressed in the sentence. We usually select the correct form of the verb automatically, but, as is so often the case in English grammar, there are instances when our natural facility with our native language can let us down. To avoid the common errors in verb tense, remember to:

- use the correct form of an irregular verb;
- use the correct forms of 'lay' and 'lie';
- use will and shall correctly;
- use the perfect verb tense correctly; and
- use the present tense when writing about film, literature, and art.

Regular and irregular verbs

English verbs have three tenses: present to indicate action that is occurring in the here and now; past to indicate action that has already occurred; and future to indicate action that is to occur later on in time: I start a new book every day; I started a new book yesterday; I will start to read a new book tomorrow.

Most verbs add the suffix 'ed' to indicate past: started, finished, conquered. This verb form—with the 'ed' suffix—is used to indicate simple past (I started) or to indicate more complex forms of the past and future, those form that include auxiliary or helping verbs: I have started to read a new book today; I had just started to read a new book, when my doorbell rang; If I start a new book today, I will have started four new books this week. These verbs that add 'ed' are called **regular verbs**. A regular verb is one that forms its past and past participle by adding the suffix 'ed'. The past participle is the form of the verb that is used when a helping verb is added to convey more complex temporal relationships within a sentence: have started, had started, will have started.

But there are nearly one hundred common English verbs that form their past tense and their past participle in other ways. We write 'I started to read a new book yesterday,' but not 'I beginned to read a new book yesterday'. The past tense of the verb 'begin' is, of course, 'began': 'I began to read a new book yesterday'. To add to the challenge, we cannot write 'I have began to read a new book today'. The past participle form of this verb, that form that is used with an auxiliary verb, is 'begun': 'I have begun to read a new book today'. These verbs that do not add 'ed' to form their past and past participle forms are called irregular verbs. Here are ten sentences, all of which contain errors in verb tense, caused by the misuse of an irregular verb.

1. He had broke all of his vows.
2. I have not boughten a new pair of shoes since last May.
3. Alice has chose to attend the University of London.
4. She had drove for nearly ten hours without stopping.
5. Harry had drank eight pints of bitter and needed a ride home.
6. If we had knowed then what we know now, we would not have bought the house.
7. Their bodies were found on Friday, but it was clear that they had froze and perished days earlier.
8. The money was hid in a hole in the basement.
9. I seen the movie three times and still it moves me.
10. The Queen has rode the same horse for the past four years.

Here are the sentences again, with the correct form of the irregular verb:

1. He had broken all of his vows.
2. I have not bought a new pair of shoes since last May.
3. Alice has chosen to attend the University of London.
4. She had driven for nearly ten hours without stopping.
5. Harry had drunk eight pints of bitter and needed a ride home.
6. If we had known then what we know now, we would not have bought the house.
7. Their bodies were found on Friday, but it was clear that they had frozen and perished days earlier.
8. The money was hidden in a hole in the basement.
9. I have seen the movie three times and still it moves me.
10. The Queen has ridden the same horse for the past four years.

It is not always easy to select the correct form of an irregular verb. They are, by definition, inconsistent in form. Some irregular verbs take three different forms for present, past, and past participle: arise, arose, arisen; begin, began, begun; blow, blew, blown; break, broke, broken; choose, chose, chosen; do, did, done; draw, drew, drawn; drink, drank, drunk; drive, drove, driven; eat, ate, eaten; fall, fell, fallen; fly, flew, flown; freeze, froze, frozen; give, gave, given; go, went, gone; grow, grew, grown; hide, hid, hidden; know, knew, known; lie, lay, lain; ride, rode, ridden; ring, rang, rung; see, saw, seen; shake, shook, shaken; shrink, shrank, shrunk; sing, sang, sung; sink, sank, sunk; slay, slew, slain; speak, spoke, spoken; spring, sprang, sprung; steal, stole, stolen; swear, swore, sworn; swim, swan, swum; take, took, taken; throw, threw, thrown; wear, wore, worn; and write, wrote, written.

Some irregular verbs have two words—both of which are correct—that can be used to denote the past or past participle forms: awake, awoke or awaked; beat, beat, beat or beaten; bite, bit, bitten or bit; dive, dived or dove, dived; dream, dreamed or dreamt; dreamed or dreamt; forget, forgot, forgot or forgotten; get, got, got or gotten; prove, proved, proved or proven; strike, struck, struck or stricken; and wake, woke or waked; waked or woken.

Some irregular verbs, like regular verbs but without the 'ed' suffix, use the same form for the past and past participle tenses: bent, brought, built, caught, clung, dealt, dug, dragged, fought, found, hung (i.e. suspended), hanged (i.e. executed), had, heard, kept, laid (i.e. put), led, lent, lost, made, said, sent, shot, sat, slept, spun, stood, stung, swung, taught, and wrung.

Finally, some irregular verbs use the same word to denote all three forms: burst, cost, let, and set. The verb 'read' also uses the same word for all forms but the pronunciation changes, from 'reed' in the present to 'red' for the past and past participle tenses.

Three forms of some irregular verbs; two forms, both of which can form the past and past participle; one word for both past and past participle; and one word to denote present, past, and past participle: This is too much to remember about irregular verbs. Fortunately, we have a valuable ally in our goal to always use irregular verbs correctly. A good dictionary will indicate if a verb is irregular and will provide its three forms. Many excellent dictionaries are online now, and you can use them without charge. Here is the entry and the first definition for 'write' from the Cambridge English Dictionary Online (http://dictionary.cambridge.org). Note how prominently the past and past participle forms are displayed.

Write show phonetics

verb **wrote**, **written** or OLD USE **writ**

1 [I or T] to make marks which represent letters, words or numbers on a surface, such as paper or a computer screen, using a pen, pencil or keyboard, or to use this method to record thoughts, facts or messages:

When you fill in the form, please write ***clearly/legibly*** *in black ink.*

[+ speech] "I hope to see you next Saturday," she wrote.

Why not write ***(down)*** *your ideas on a piece of paper before you start?*

Here is the entry for the verb 'sleep'. Notice that the entry includes both the past and past participle forms, even though they are the same.

Sleep show phonetics

verb **slept, slept**

1 [I] to be in the state of rest when your eyes are closed, your body is not active, and your mind is unconscious:

I couldn't sleep because of all the noise next door.

I slept ***late*** *on Sunday morning.*

How can Jayne sleep ***at night*** *with all those worries on her mind!*

We had dinner with Ann and Charles and slept ***the night*** *(with them)* (= at their home).

To lay and to lie

Two irregular verbs that often cause even experienced writers to reach for the dictionary are the verbs 'to lay' and 'to lie' (as in recline, not misrepresent). These verbs are confusing because the present tense of 'to lay' is the same word as the past tense of 'to lie'. Moreover, the verb 'to lie' has three different words to represent present, past, and past participle: lie, lay, lain. The verb 'to lay' uses one word 'laid' to represent both the past and past participle forms. Study these sentences carefully:

As long as I can lie down, I can sleep anywhere.
She lay in bed all day, feeling too sick to move.
She has lain in bed, barely moving, for the past two days.

These sentences illustrate the three forms—present, past, and past participle—of the irregular verb 'to lie'.

Study these sentences carefully:

You can lay your head on my shoulder and go to sleep.
She laid her head on my shoulder and promptly fell asleep.
She would have slept, if she had laid her head on my shoulder.

These sentences illustrate the three forms—present, past, and past participle—of the irregular verb 'to lay'.

Do you notice anything that distinguishes the two sets of sentences above, other than the fact that they use the three forms of two different verbs? Notice that the 'to lie' sentences do not contain direct objects, while the 'to lay' sentences do: lay your head, laid her head, had laid her head. Here is the key distinction between 'lay' and 'lie': The verb 'to lie' does not take a direct object; the verb 'to lay' does. In other words, if you have to choose between lay and lie, you can do so by determining whether or not the verb is followed by a direct object. If it is, choose a form of lay; if it is not, choose a form of lie.

Consider these sentences:

Every night, she lies on the sofa and falls asleep.
Every night, she lays her kitten on the sofa and falls asleep beside it.

Last night, she lay on the sofa and fell asleep.
Last night, she laid her kitten on the sofa and fell asleep beside it.

For the past three nights, she has lain on the sofa and fallen asleep there.
For the past three nights, she has laid her kitten on the sofa and fallen asleep beside it.

These sentence pairs illustrate the three forms of the two verbs. The first sentence pair illustrates the present-tense use of the verbs; the second pair, the past tense; the third pair, the past participle. Why is the 'to lay' form of the verb required in the second sentence in each pair? The 'to lay' form is required because of the presence of the direct object 'kitten'.

Note that this direct-object/no-direct-object distinction applies, as well, to the 'ing' forms of the two verbs:

She is lying on the sofa, and, soon, she will fall asleep.
Now she is laying her kitten on the sofa, and, soon, she will fall asleep beside it.

Will and shall

Generally speaking, the rules of Standard English and Edited American English are the same. One way in which they differ, though, is in the use of the auxiliary verbs 'will' and 'shall'. In British English, 'I shall' and 'we shall' are used to express the simple future:

I shall catch the streetcar named Desire.
We shall take the morning train.

Americans seem to think the use of 'shall' in such contexts is an affectation and would use 'will' or, less formally, would contract the verb: I'll catch the streetcar named Desire. British English prescribes the use of 'will' to express determination, even in the first person: I will not ride in a streetcar.

Conversely, British English prescribes the use of 'shall' to express determination when the subject is in the second or third person:

Eleanor shall know the full extent of my wrath, if she disobeys another order.
She shall never surrender.

American writers would use 'will' in these sentences.

Edited American English does prescribe the use of 'shall' when the use of 'will' would be semantically inappropriate:

Shall I bring my own tools?
Shall we dance?

According to *The New Fowler's* (p. 706) the use of 'shall' is becoming less frequent, even in British English usage.

Perfect verb tense

The perfect tense of English verbs are those that include a form of the verb 'to have' as an auxiliary verb. Like all verbs, it has three tenses, present, past, and future. Consider these sentences:

I have written you a letter.
Evan has written a new novel.

I thought I had written to you already.
Evan had written the entire novel by the time the plane landed.

Evan never writes to me, but, if I write him a letter today, I will have written him a letter every day this week.

If he writes a new novel this year, Evan will have written a novel a year for the past five years.

The first sentence pair illustrates the use of the present perfect tense of the verb 'to write'. The second sentence pair illustrates the use of the past perfect tense of the verb 'to write'. The third sentence pair illustrates the use of the future perfect tense of the verb 'to write'.

In English, we use the perfect verb tense to establish precise temporal relationships among the subjects and objects in a sentence. What is the difference in meaning between these two sentences:

I have written you a letter.

I wrote you a letter.

Both sentence verbs denote a past action, but the first sentence verb denotes a more present past action than the second. When you say 'I have taken my shower' you are suggesting a more recent event than you would when you say 'I took my shower'. Similarly, compare 'I have taken my shower; you can take yours now, if you like' to 'I took my shower an hour ago'.

What is the difference in meaning between these two sentences:

Evan has written a new novel.

Evan wrote a new novel.

Again, the verb in the first sentence connotes a more recent past even than does the verb in the second sentence. You could say 'Evan wrote a new novel last year', but you would not say 'Evan has written a new novel last year'. To connote a continuous activity, you would also use the present perfect tense: 'Evan has written a new novel every year for the past five years', but not 'Evan wrote a new novel every year for the past five years'. The present perfect tense is also used for emphasis: 'Wendy is wrong; Evan has written a new novel'.

What is the difference in meaning between these two sentences:

> I thought I had written to you already.
> I thought I wrote to you already.

Both sentences indicate a past action, but the verb in the first sentence connotes an action that took place in the more recent past. The past perfect is often used in the context of some other action, usually action taking place in the immediate past. This sentence contains a subtle error in verb tense:

> Everyone was complaining about the weather, but I never saw snow before, so I was thrilled.

The error here is that the simple past tense 'saw' is used, but because of the 'complaining' taking place in the immediate past, the past perfect form is required.

> Everyone was complaining about the weather, but I <u>had never seen</u> snow before, so I was thrilled.

These sentences also illustrate the difference between the simple past and the past perfect verb forms. Note how the temporal context of events that take place in other parts of the sentence influence the distinction between the simple past and the past perfect tenses. The inclusion of negative adverbs, such as 'not' or 'never' often influence the tense choice.

> I forgot the formula, so I answered question three incorrectly.
>
> If I had not forgotten the formula, I would have answered question three correctly.
>
> Napoleon surrendered just after midnight, and, by sunrise, they had the dispatch that confirmed he had, indeed, surrendered.

This distinction between the use of the simple past and the past perfect can be subtle. When you edit your writing, check closely your past tense verbs to make certain they should not be switched to past perfect.

What, finally, is the difference in meaning between these two sentences:

> Evan will write a new novel next year.
> If he writes a new novel this year, Evan will have written a novel a year for the past five years.

Clearly, the first sentence is simple present, and its verb denotes an action that will occur in the future. The second sentence is more complex. The subordinate clause 'If he writes a new novel this year' combined with the continuous past action ('the past five years') specified at the end of the sentence dictates the use of the future perfect verb tense 'will have written'. The 'if' clause alone does not dictate the use of the future perfect, as this sentence illustrates: If Evan writes a new novel this year, his publisher will celebrate. In this sentence, the future perfect 'will have celebrated' would be wrong because there are no conditions that would dictate its use. Consider these sentences:

> If we win again tomorrow, Arsenal will win four consecutive games.
> By the time we land at Heathrow, I will read Evan's new novel.
> If the Prime Minister fires the Minister of Defence, she will fire three cabinet ministers since she came to power.

All of these sentences contain an error in verb tense. The writer has used simple present 'will win', 'will read', and 'will fire', but conditions established within the sentences dictate the use of the future perfect tense. Note that all of the conditions, of winning, landing, and firing, are expressed in the present tense. Corrected, the sentences will read:

> If we win again tomorrow, Arsenal will have won four consecutive games.
> By the time we land at Heathrow, I will have read Evan's new novel.

If the Prime Minister fires the Minister of Defence, she <u>will have fired</u> three cabinet ministers since she came to power.

A digression: Verb mood and voice

As this Chapter makes clear, verbs have many tenses. In addition to simple present, past, and future (I sing today, I sang yesterday, and I will sing tomorrow), there are perfect tense to indicate more complex temporal relationships (I have sung that hymn in church for the past four Sundays) and progressive tense, to indicate ongoing action (I am singing that hymn today, I was singing it yesterday, and I will be singing it tomorrow). Indeed, perfect and progressive tenses combine, often to signal ongoing past action in the context of some other present action (She has been singing the same hymn in church for the past four Sundays, and the congregation is beginning to tire of it).

In addition to tense, verbs have **mood**. **Indicative** mood is by far the most common, used as it is to express regular, normal action. **Imperative** mood expresses a command and is sometimes used with an understood rather than a specifically stated subject: Get out of here! And stay away from me! **Subjunctive** mood is the trickiest, and you need to remember two rules to use it correctly.

First, use subjunctive mood when you want to express a condition contrary to fact. Compare these two sentences:

Viscount Parfitt-James was a rich man, and many women were attracted to him, in spite of his less-than-perfect physical appearance.

If Viscount Parfitt-James were a rich man, more women might be attracted to him.

The second sentence presents a hypothesis which is not true and uses, therefore, the subjunctive mood form of the verb.

Second, use subjunctive mood to express an order or a recommendation, often those contained within a noun clause. Compare these sentence pairs:

We hope the defendant <u>receives</u> a stiff jail sentence.

The jury insisted that the defendant <u>receive</u> a stiff jail sentence.

She <u>sees</u> a specialist once a month.

Dr. Johnson recommended that she <u>see</u> a specialist.

The first sentence in each pair is in indicative mood, but in the second sentences a noun clause follows an order or recommendation. The subjunctive mood (typically the form without the 's' at the end) is used for the verb in these clauses. In sentences that require a form of the verb 'to be' in a 'that' clause, the word 'be' forms the subjunctive. Compare:

Effective May 1st the policy is rescinded.

Council recommended that the policy <u>be</u> rescinded.

Verbs also have <u>voice</u>, which helps to establish the relationship in a sentence between the subject and the object. In the more commonly used <u>active voice</u> sentence the subject is the doing something: My dentist won the lottery. In a <u>passive voice</u> sentence the active-voice subject becomes acted upon: The lottery was won by my dentist. The passive voice is useful when the subject is indeterminate: Smoking is forbidden in this building; She is reputed to be a diva. But, as a general rule, active voice is preferable because it is more concise. In the sentence you have just read, the first verb—active voice <u>is preferable</u>—is in passive voice and the second—it <u>is</u>—is in active voice. In only active voice the sentence would read: readers prefer active voice because it is more concise. (See also Chapter Four.)

Tense and when writing about works of art and literature

When you are writing about a dead author or artist's life, you use, of course, the past tense of the verb: Keats was born in London; Shakespeare died in 1616. But no matter how long ago a book was written or an artwork was painted, the rules of Standard English prescribe the use of the present tense of the verb when you analyse or discuss works of art and literature. The following sentences use the present tense of the verb correctly.

> Jane Austen characterises Elizabeth as an assertive and free-spirited young woman who refuses to let Darcy's arrogance go unchallenged.
>
> Hamlet's tragic flaw is, in part, his inability to act, but he does react spontaneously and rashly when he challenges Laertes at Ophelia's funeral.
>
> In Constable's best work, the light shimmers and reflects off the water, in a manner the eye recognises as, at once, real and surreal.
>
> The cartoon depicts two scarecrows in open farmland, but the scarecrows are real people, one turning to the other and saying 'English lit … how about you'?

Tutorial

Progress questions

Revise the following sentences to correct any verb tense errors you detect.

1. Last Thursday Em read that prolonged insomnia can adversely affect a person's heath and ever since then she sleeps until noon.
2. Sleep apnoea is a disorder that occurs when air passages are blocked, causing the sleeper to stop breathing until the associated discomfort forced him or her to awaken suddenly.
3. The presence of thousand of new patients at sleep clinics each year suggest that sleep disorders are becoming more common.
4. Medical schools do not offer specialties in sleep medicine, but, as more and more research confirms a link between sleep and good health, they have to consider offering that option.
5. For the past three years, she failed to get enough sleep, and now her health is at risk.
6. He had took naps while he was at work, but he won his wrongful dismissal case when his lawyer cited research suggesting that an afternoon nap can cut the risk of heart disease
7. The accident occurred because he fell asleep at the wheel, but he had drove all night to get to Canterbury in time.
8. It was well after midnight, and, still, she was laying in bed, trying to fall asleep.
9. She had laid in bed for so long that she was worried her muscles might began to atrophy.
10. Pip's epiphany came when he realised that Joe's selflessness and humility were the traits of a true gentleman.

Define and provide, in a sentence, an example of the following terms:

1. Perfect tense
2. Progressive tense

3. Subjunctive mood
4. Irregular verb
5. Perfect progressive tense.

Discussion point

What is the difference in meaning between the past tense and the past perfect tense? What is the difference in meaning between the past tense and the present perfect tense? What is the difference in meaning between the present tense and the present progressive tense?

Practical assignment

Write twelve sentences, one to illustrate each of the twelve verb tenses, i.e. present, past, future, present progressive, past progressive, future progressive, present perfect, past perfect, future perfect, present perfect progressive, past perfect progressive, and future perfect progressive.

Study and revision tip

Remember that a good dictionary will list all three forms of irregular verbs.

Answers to the progress questions

Revise the following sentences to correct any verb tense errors you detect.

1. Last Thursday Em read that prolonged insomnia can adversely affect a person's heath and ever since then she <u>has slept</u> until noon.
2. Sleep apnoea is a disorder that occurs when air passages are blocked, causing the sleeper to stop breathing until the associated discomfort <u>forces</u> him or her to awaken suddenly.
3. The presence of thousand of new patients at sleep clinics each year <u>suggests</u> that sleep disorders are becoming more common.
4. Medical schools do not offer specialties in sleep medicine, but, as more and more research confirms a link between sleep and good health, they <u>will have</u> to consider offering that option.

5. For the past three years, she has failed to get enough sleep, and now her health is at risk.
6. He had taken naps while he was at work, but he won his wrongful dismissal case when his lawyer cited research suggesting that an afternoon nap can cut the risk of heart disease
7. The accident occurred because he fell asleep at the wheel, but he had driven all night to get to Canterbury in time.
8. It was well after midnight, and, still, she was lying in bed, trying to fall asleep.
9. She had lain in bed for so long that she was worried her muscles might begin to atrophy.
10. Pip's epiphany comes when he realises that Joe's selflessness and humility are the traits of a true gentleman.

Define and provide, in a sentence, an example of the following terms.

1. Perfect tense is the form of the verb that uses a form of the verb 'to have' as an auxiliary: I have wasted too much time; I had wasted too much time; I will have wasted too much time.
2. Progressive tense is any form of a verb that uses the 'ing' suffix: I am wasting too much time; I was wasting too much time; I will be wasting too much time.
3. Subjunctive mood is a verb form used in 'that' clauses that contain a recommendation or condition and in sentences that state a condition contrary to fact: If I were driving the children would be safe; I had to insist she drive carefully.
4. An irregular verb is one that changes form in a way other than adding 'ed' to indicate past and past participle forms: You threw the ball much too fast, and you have thrown in that way before, but I will throw the ball to you more slowly.
5. Perfect progressive tense combines a form of the verb 'to have' as a helping verb with the 'ing' form of a main verb: I have been brushing my teeth with my finger for many years; before the dentist ordered me to stop, I had been brushing my teeth with my finger for many years; if I brush my teeth with my finger again next year, I will have been brushing my teeth with my finger for the past five years.

9 Grammar and punctuation

One-minute summary

In some sentences, proper grammar relies on proper punctuation. In Chapter Three, for example, you learned that a comma is not considered a strong enough punctuation mark to separate two complete sentences, that a period or a semi-colon is usually required instead. In this Chapter, we will review those punctuation/grammar rules we have covered already and learn other grammar rules that rely upon the correct use of punctuation marks. Specifically, this Chapter covers:

- The use of the semi-colon between two sentences.
- The use of the comma to separate non-essential words, phrases, and clauses from the rest of a sentence.
- The use of the comma between coordinate adjectives.
- The use of the comma or semi-colon for words, phrases, or clauses in a series.

When to use a semi-colon between sentences

The full stop or period normally signals the end of a sentence. A comma does not; it is not considered to be a strong enough signal with which to end a sentence. As you learned in Chapter Three, two sentences separated only by a comma commit the grammar infraction known as the run-on sentence or, as it is sometimes called, the comma splice. Here are two examples:

> Coffee in specialty restaurants is expensive, upscale coffee shops charge as much as £3 for a cup of coffee, blended with all manner of syrups and milks.
>
> The English place a trunk call to their solicitors, Americans place a long-distance call to their lawyers.

The first sentence contains two commas, but note that the first comma separates two complete sentences and is therefore used incorrectly. A full stop could be used here, but since the two sentences are so closely related in meaning—and note that the key word 'coffee' appears at the start of each one—a semi-colon might be even more appropriate. The second comma is fine, in that it precedes not a complete sentence but a phrase that modifies 'coffee'. The second sentence could also be reduced to a phrase to correct the error, in which case the sentence would read:

> Coffee in specialty restaurants is expensive, with upscale coffee shops charging as much as £3 for a cup of coffee, blended with all manner of syrups and milks.

The second sentence is also incorrect, it is a run-on sentence. Again a full stop could replace the comma, but, since the two sentences are related in meaning and parallel in structure (see Chapter Four), a semi-colon would be effective. The comma would be correct if one of the sentences became a subordinate clause. Start either sentence with the word 'while', for example, and the sentence is grammatically correct.

> While the English place a trunk call to their solicitors, Americans place a long-distance call to their lawyers.
>
> The English place a trunk call to their solicitors, while Americans place a long-distance call to their lawyers.

Remember as well, from Chapter Three, that a colon can also separate two complete sentences, when the second sentence elaborates upon a point stated or implied in the first:

> The new vocabulary was confusing so he explained it a third time: The English place a trunk call to their solicitors, while Americans place a long-distance call to their lawyers.
>
> I will give you proof that the coffee at Moons is expensive: I just paid £3 for a medium latte flavoured with soy milk and caramel syrup!

Commas separate non-essential words, phrases, and clauses

Study this sentence carefully:

> Bordeaux, in the south of France, is a popular vacation destination, especially for Europeans.

Notice that the two phrases 'in the south of France' and 'especially for Europeans' are separated from the rest of the sentence by commas. This is so because they are not essential to the sentence's meaning. Remove them and you would have a sentence that may be less specific but that still makes logical sense.

> Bordeaux is a popular vacation destination.

The phrases that have been removed are called, in the context of the rules that govern the use of the comma, non-essential or, as they are sometimes called, non-restrictive because they do not 'restrict' the meaning of the sentence.

Now study this sentence carefully:

> The only inhabited island in the Southern Archipelago is St. Pierre.

Notice that the phrase 'in the southern archipelago' is not separated from the rest of the sentence by commas. This is because it is essential to the meaning of the sentence. It is an essential or 'restrictive' phrase. Remove it and the sentence no longer makes logical sense:

> The only inhabited island is St. Pierre.

Obviously, there are other inhabited islands in the world. The phrase 'in the southern archipelago' is restrictive and, therefore, cannot be separated from the rest of the sentence by commas.

Prior context might, of course, make this sentence perfectly logical: There are many uninhabited islands in the southern archipelago; in fact, the only inhabited island is St. Pierre. Moreover, the restrictive/non-restrictive distinction is often ignored when the phrase is at the beginning of the sentence. In this sentence, the use of the comma would be optional.

In the southern archipelago, the only inhabited island is St. Pierre.

As a rule, though, knowing the distinction between restrictive and non-restrictive elements will help you use the comma correctly.

Here are three more sentences that use commas to separate non-restrictive elements from the rest of the sentence:

Dickens' first novel, *The Pickwick Papers*, is still on the syllabus.
For her riding class, I must buy my daughter Lucci boots, which are very expensive.
My father, his attention distracted by the glare of the sun, sideswiped the blue Mercedes.

Here are three more sentences that do not use commas because the sentences contain restrictive phrases or clauses.

The witness identified the girl in the blue suit as the accomplice.
The company was famous for making clothes that were durable.
All of the books related to my topic were signed out by someone else.

Note that the distinction between a restrictive and non-restrictive element is not always cut and dried. In such instances, you, as the writer, decide whether or not you want the comma. My grammar check is asking me if I want to delete the comma in this sentence:

Moons charges as much as £3 for a cup of coffee, blended with chocolate milk and caramel syrup.

But I don't. I think the phrase following the comma is non-essential, so I choose to leave the comma in.

Note, also, that some grammarians insist that the word 'that' conventionally introduces a restrictive noun clause, while the word 'which' conventionally introduces a non-restrictive clause. No comma would precede 'that', then, but a comma would precede 'which'. Other grammarians argue that this distinction is far from absolute.

Note, finally, that the inclusion or exclusion of a comma might come with certain connotations. In this sentence, the noun Frank could or could not be separated from the rest of the sentence with commas: My neighbour's son (,) Frank (,) is serving with the SAS in Iraq. If commas are included, the implication is that my neighbour has only one son. If the commas are excluded, the implication is that my neighbour has more than one son and the writer is restricting the meaning of the sentence to the one son serving in Iraq.

The comma between coordinate adjectives

In Chapter One, you learned that an adjective is a word that modifies, defines, enhances a noun: <u>simple</u> pleasures, <u>Rosetta</u> stone, <u>old</u> man, <u>light</u> opera, <u>starry</u> nights. When two adjectives precede a noun, they might be coordinate or cumulative adjectives. Coordinate adjectives clearly and separately modify the noun—they could be separated by the conjunction 'and': the long and winding road; the long, winding road. Cumulative adjectives build upon each other, the first on the second, so that, although they both modify the noun, the first almost seems to be modifying the second, which, in turn, modifies the noun. The conjunction 'and' would not work between them: blue suede shoes, one fine day, formal dinner party.

The rule is this: a comma comes between coordinate adjectives but not between cumulative adjectives. Note the punctuation of the following phrases:

Pleasant, unexpected surprise
Fried green tomatoes
Dull, poorly written novel
Sweet apple pie

Words, phrases, and clauses in a series

Words, phrases, and clauses in a parallel series are usually separated from each other by commas. Consider these sentences, the first of which contains words in a series, the second of which contains phrases in a series, and the third of which contains clauses in a series:

> Some enchanted evening, you may meet a tall, dark, rich, and handsome stranger.
> We went to the airport by bus, to Liverpool by plane, across the Mersey by ferry, and to his flat by car.
> Consider these sentences, the first of which contains words in a series, the second of which contains phrases in a series, and the third of which contains clauses in a series.

Note that, in all sentences, there is a comma after the second-to-last item in the series, followed by the word 'and', followed by the last item in the series. This last comma—known as the serial comma—is optional, though it is usually included in British English and omitted in American English.

Note that if phrases or, more likely, clauses in a series contain commas within them, then they are separated from each other by semi-colons. Study carefully these three examples:

> The Hemingway stories on the reading list are 'Hills Like White Elephants', from *Men Without Women*, published in 1927; 'A Clean Well-Lighted Place', from *Winner Take Nothing*, published in 1933; and 'The Snows of Kilimanjaro', published in the August, 1936 issue of *Esquire*.

> She already has an English setter, who is old and infirm; a black labrador, with the energy of a dynamo; and a border collie, who rivals Houdini, as an escape artist, so she reluctantly decided she could not take one of Millie's puppies.

We had a thirty-minute stopover in Chicago, but we were not allowed to deplane; an hour stop in Minneapolis, where we were allowed to deplane, but only for fifteen minutes; and another thirty-minute stop in Seattle, where, again, we were not allowed to leave the aircraft.

Tutorial

Progress questions

Revise the following sentences to correct punctuation errors you detect.

1. Two glasses of red wine with dinner has beneficial effects, for a man; but a woman should drink just one glass to get the same health benefits.
2. A mega-store which put our hardware store and grocery store out of business was built just north of our county town.
3. Chocolate is made from the kernels of fermented roasted cocoa beans.
4. Chocolate is rich in carbohydrates, it also contains small amounts of caffeine.
5. The cocoa bean was first used like the coffee bean to make a bitter hot drink
6. Hernan Cortes drank cocoa when he explored Mexico for the King of Spain, he brought beans home to Spain which began to import them.
7. In Spain cocoa connoisseurs spiced up their hot chocolate adding sugar cinnamon and vanilla.
8. Chocolate was an expensive, delicacy in 17th century Europe.
9. The cocoa bean can be ground to form a paste, which is often hardened into chunks to produce baking chocolate, pressed to make cocoa powder, or mixed with sugar and milk to make bitter or sweet chocolate—the amount of sugar and milk determines the taste—for immediate consumption.
10. Some consider dark chocolate a health food because it contains flavonoids which are good for the heart, the high fat content of milk chocolate negates all of chocolate's healthy ingredients.

Define and provide, in a sentence, an example of the following terms:

1. Coordinate adjectives

2. Cumulative adjectives
3. Restrictive phrase or clause
4. Non-restrictive phrase or clause.

Discussion point

How does proper punctuation help readers understand the meaning of a written text? How can punctuation errors make it more difficult for readers to comprehend a written text?

Practical assignment

Compose and punctuate correctly a sentence that:

- illustrates the use of the semi-colon to separate two sentences;
- contains a restrictive phrase;
- contains a non-restrictive clause;
- contains coordinate adjectives;
- contains cumulative adjectives;
- contains three phrases, at least one of which has a comma or commas within it.

Study and revision tip

See the Studymates title *The Academic Essay* by Derek Soles, for a complete discussion of the rules of punctuation.

Answers to the progress questions

Revise the following sentences to correct any punctuation errors you detect.

1. Two glasses of red wine with dinner has beneficial effects for a man, but a woman should drink just one glass to get the same health benefits.
2. A mega-store, which put our hardware store and grocery store out of business, was built just north of our county town.
3. Chocolate is made from the kernels of fermented, roasted cocoa beans.
4. Chocolate is rich in carbohydrates; it also contains small amounts of caffeine.
5. The cocoa bean was first used, like the coffee bean, to make a bitter hot drink

6. Hernan Cortes drank cocoa when he explored Mexico for the King of Spain. He brought beans home to Spain which began to import them.
7. In Spain cocoa connoisseurs spiced up their hot chocolate, adding sugar cinnamon and vanilla.
8. Chocolate was an expensive delicacy in 17th century Europe.
9. The cocoa bean can be ground to form a paste, which is often hardened into chunks to produce baking chocolate; pressed to make cocoa powder; or mixed with sugar and milk to make bitter or sweet chocolate—the amount of sugar and milk determines the taste—for immediate consumption.
10. Some consider dark chocolate a health food because it contains flavonoids, which are good for the heart, but the high fat content of milk chocolate negates all of chocolate's healthy ingredients.

Define and provide, in a sentence, an example of the following terms.

Examples will vary.

1. Coordinate adjectives: those that modify a noun independently and that are, therefore, separated from each other by commas. A fierce, destructive tornado ripped through a small Kansas town.
2. Cumulative adjectives: those, usually in a pair, not separated by commas; the first adjective qualifies the second which modifies the noun. When there is a dark green tinge in a Kansas sky, it might signal the presence of a tornado.
3. Restrictive phrase or clause. One essential to the meaning of the sentence and, therefore, not marked off from the sentence by commas. The tornados that begin in Oklahoma often gain steam as they move north to Kansas.
4. Non-restrictive phrase or clause. One not essential to the meaning of the sentence and, therefore, marked off from the sentence by commas. The May 1, 1944 tornado, which began life as a heavy Oklahoma wind, moved north rapidly and destroyed half of a small southern Kansas farming town.

10 Grammar and usage

One-minute summary

Grammar and usage are two interrelated but slightly different branches of speech and rhetoric. Grammar is a system of rules that governs the selection and arrangement of words in sentences. Usage has more to do with correct word choice in correct context, on the choice, for example, between affect or effect, already or all ready, bad or badly, bring or take. This choice, though, often depends upon the part of speech—noun, verb, modifier—the word represents. In this sense, then, grammar and usage unite and a grammar primer must include some instruction in usage, insofar as usage is determined by grammar rules that govern nouns, verbs, and modifiers. The purpose of this Chapter is to cover those rules of usage that are contingent upon some rules of grammar, those rules, especially, that clarify:

- Nouns and pronouns frequently misused.
- Verbs frequently misused.
- Modifiers frequently misused.

Nouns and pronouns frequently misused

Here, in alphabetical order, are some nouns and pronouns frequently misused and an explanation of how to use them correctly.

Allusion: This means in reference to, as distinct from its homonym *illusion*, which means false vision: He made many allusions to *The Tempest*, a play filled with striking visions and optical illusions.

Any one: This phrase refers to one person as distinct from *anyone*, which refers to more than one: Any one of the children in her class could have told the hikers that anyone who hoped to make it as far a Katmandu in one day is going to be disappointed.

Data: Traditionally the plural form of datum, but now regularly used as the singular and form of the noun: The data is ambiguous.

Effect: This noun causes confusion because there is one verb that has an identical spelling and another (affect) that has the same pronunciation. As a noun, effect is synonymous with impact or end product: she has a soothing <u>effect</u> on me. As a verb, spelled the same way, it is synonymous with achieve or bring about: Her book will effect a change in policy. As a verb beginning with 'a', affect means influence (Her good looks will affect his decision) or pretend to have (She affects indifference).

Every one: similar to *any one* (above) this phrase refers to one person, as distinct from *everyone*, which refers to more than one: Every one of the union leaders claimed that everyone attended the rally.

It's, its: It's is a contraction for it is, as distinct from its, which is a possessive pronoun: It's missing one of its pages. It can be found quite often where writers believe the possessive form must take an apostrophe, but there is no such word as its'.

Mankind: Some editors and English teachers consider this noun sexist and prefer humankind or humanity to be used in its stead.

Media, medium: The former is the plural form of the noun; the latter, the singular. The media hounds celebrities because the public wants to hear all about the lives of the rich and famous; one medium that shows some restraint is BBC Radio.

Moral, morale: The former means lesson or upright conduct; the latter, mood. The moral of the report is that employee morale will remain low if wages don't improve.

Myself: An intensive—I myself would never do it—or reflective—I will do it myself—pronoun. Use me as object of a preposition—Give it David or me (not myself)—and I as the subject of a verb—Jenny and I (not myself) are tired.

Number: 'The' number usually takes a singular verb; 'a' number usually takes a plural verb. The number of students attending university is on the rise. A number of items are missing.

Per cent, percentage: Per cent is used with a specific number, while percentage is a general measure. Over sixty per cent of the students at Newton are scholarship winners; the percentage is even higher at Bodkin.

Principal, principle: Principal is a noun meaning top administrator or an adjective meaning essential, as distinct from principle, meaning guiding truth. Her principal reason for refusing to vote was that none of the candidates supported the economic principles she thought were needed to end the recession.

Who, which, that: Use who in reference to people. The prisoners who (not that or which) rioted will be punished.

Verbs frequently misused

Here, in alphabetical order, are some verbs frequently misused and an explanation of how to use them correctly.

Affect: This verb is a homonym for the noun 'effect' (q.v.) and for the verb 'effect' (q.v.), so it is sometimes misused. It means to influence: The rejection letter affected her mood; (it had a negative effect upon her).

Awake: Interchangeable with 'wake' though after 'up', 'wake' is used: I (a)wake every morning at five.

Allude: This verb means to refer to, as distinct from its homonym *elude* which means to escape from: The study he alluded to in his speech was done almost twenty-five years ago, but Professor Schick eluded criticism by convincing us that its findings are still relevant.

Can: In formal English, can always implied ability to act, while *may* implied permission to act. I can come; may

I come? *Can* is often used informally in the same context as *may*: Yes, you can come.

Complement: The verb meaning to go with or to complete; not to be confused with to *compliment*, meaning to praise: The colour of your tie complements the colour of your shirt. Thank you for the compliment.

Could of: Misuse of could have. I could have danced all night.

Effect: This verb sometimes causes confusion because there is a noun with the identical spelling (q.v.) and another verb different only in its first letter: affect (q.v.). As a verb, to effect means to bring about: The foul affected her play; it had a negative effect; but it underscored the need to effect change in the way the game is played.

Ensure: to ensure means to make certain, as distinct form 'to insure' which usually involves financial protection. In American English,'insure' is sometimes used interchangeably with 'ensure'.

Imply, infer: Imply denotes suggestions, as distinct from infer which denotes conclusions drawn from evidence. It's safe to infer that much of Yeats' poetry is autobiographical, but I'm not implying his work is more autobiographical than Auden's.

Hung, hanged: Hung is the more frequently used past participle for 'to hang'; hanged is used in the context of capital punishment. Many years ago they hanged even pickpockets.

Lead, led: The latter is the past tense and participle of the verb to lead. William led us to victory, but Harry will lead the party.

Lend, loan: Lend is a verb, as distinct from loan which is a noun. If you lend me five pounds, I'll repay the loan within a week.

Lose: Be careful not to confuse this verb meaning misplace with the adjective *loose*, meaning subject to dispersal. I did not lose all of my money, just some loose change in my jacket pocket.

May: see *can* above.

Passed: A verb (Today, I passed you on the street) not to be confused with 'past', which can be a noun (His past came back to haunt him) or an adjective (a past life; a past mistake).

Precede, proceed: To precede means to go ahead of, as distinct from to proceed, which means to continue going forward. Our visit to Newcastle preceded our visit to Edinburgh, after which we proceeded to Dublin.

Raise, rise: To raise is a transitive verb and, as such, takes a direct object; to rise (rose, risen) is an intransitive verb and, as such, does not. After they raised taxes, the stock market rose.

Used to: The d is silent but necessary. I'm getting used to (not use to) delays at airports.

Modifiers frequently misused

Here, in alphabetical order, are some adjectives, adverbs, prepositions, and conjunctions frequently misused and an explanation of how to use them correctly.

Adverse: This adjective means unfavourable: adverse weather conditions. Do not confuse it with the adjective 'averse', which means reluctant: averse to bad weather.

Afterward(s): this adverb can be used with or without the 's', though the form without the 's' is especially common in North American English.

Altogether: This adverb means complete or total: it was an altogether happy time. It is distinct from 'all together', which consists of a separate indefinite pronoun followed by an adverb: We were all together again at last. The same distinction applies to *already* and *all ready*: It was already past ten but the band was not all ready to perform.

Amid: Interchangeable with amidst but more common: Amid(st) the chaos of the protest march, we became separated. *Among*, similarly, is more commonly used than *amongst*.

Among: see *Between* below.

As: see *like* below.

Averse: see *Adverse*, above.

Awful: This word is an adjective (an awful mistake, an awful predicament) as distinct from the adverb *awfully* (awfully good to see you, an awfully beautiful county).

Backward(s): As an adverb this word is correct with or without the 's': He ran backward(s); as an adjective, the 's' is dropped: a backward glance.

Badly: This word is often misused after the linking verb *feel*. The correct use is I feel bad about that, not I feel badly about that. The adverb form is correct as a modifier for a regular verb: I played that hand badly; she behaved badly. But *feel* is a linking verb, as is the verb *to be*. It is as incorrect to write I feel badly as it would be to write I am badly. They played so badly in the first half, we felt bad for them.

Between: As a general rule, 'between' is used in divisions involving two, while *among* is used for more than two: The estate was divided evenly between the two brothers; the estate was divided evenly among the three brothers. But between is standard in some contexts: He divided his time between writing, teaching, and sailing.

Different: May be followed by 'from' or 'than' though 'different from' is more common in British English: She is our sister, but she is different from the rest of us.

Disinterested: Usually taken to mean 'impartial' as distinct from *uninterested* meaning 'not interested': He feigned disinterest, but he was concerned. I tried to explain the formula to him, but he is uninterested.

Farther, further: Farther is an adverb denoting geographical distance, as distinct from further meaning additional. There was a further delay of two hours, and then we had to re-route to Denver, which is farther away from Philadelphia than Chicago.

Fewer, less: Fewer is used with a countable quantity, less with an uncountable measure. The chemist recommended rice cakes which have fewer calories and less fat than oat squares.

Good, well: As a rule good is an adjective and well is an adverb. It was a good game because both teams played well. With 'sense' verbs, either word is correct, but the choice changes the meaning of the sentence. 'You smell good' means your fragrance is pleasing; 'you smell well' means you have a good sense of smell. With the verb 'to be', good means proficient—You are good—well connotes health—I am well.

Ingenuous, disingenuous: Ingenuous means innocent or unworldly; disingenuous means pretending to be innocent or unworldly. She is too ingenuous to see his faults, which include that disingenuous smile that fools no one else. Note that *ingenious* means shrewd or clever.

Irregardless: The first two letters are redundant, hence unnecessary.

Is when, is where: Avoid this construction when defining a term. Not 'grammar is when you study the rules of language' but 'grammar is a system of rules that govern how language is to be used'.

Like: Usually this word is a preposition (he felt like a virgin, you lie like a rug) and its use as a conjunction, in place of the preferred *as*, is frowned upon, as this sentence illustrates: She met me at the airport, like she promised she would. But its use as a conjunction is widespread and sometimes overlooked: If you knew Susan like I do, you might be suspicious, just like I said you would.

Literally: This adverb cannot be used if its verb or adjective cannot truly occur. I was literally bowled over; Jasper was literally green with envy. In both sentences, eliminate 'literally'.

Maybe: This is the adverb, as distinct from may be, which is a verb phrase. Maybe I'm right; I may be right.

Practical, practicable: Practical means sensible or useful, as distinct from practicable, meaning able to be put into practice. The Committee worked hard to develop a practical solution to the immigration problem, and they were convinced that the policy they developed was, indeed, practicable.

Real: In colloquial American speech, real is often used as an adverb (a real good time) but, in writing, it should be used only as an adjective (a real gentleman). Really is its adverb form (a really good time).

Sensuous, sensual: Sensuous refers to gratification of the senses in response to art, music, or nature, as distinct from sensual, which refers to gratification of the physical senses. Hearing Professor Kellerman read the last pages of *Ulysses* is a sensuous experience; kisses her is a sensual experience.

Some, some kind of: Not acceptable in academic writing as an adjective synonymous with excellent or wonderful. She was some pianist.

Sometime, sometimes, some time: Sometime means at an unspecified instance; sometimes means on occasion; some time means an unspecified number of seconds, minutes, hours, etc. Sometimes we dine at the Hound and Pheasant; I would like to take you there sometime. I always allow some time to pass before I switch to Cognac.

Stationary; stationery: The former is an adjective meaning at rest; the latter is writing paper and envelopes. I had to be stationary for a week due to a back injury so I bought new stationery and wrote many letters.

There, their: The former is an adverb; the latter, a possessive pronoun. We love to stay there because their beds are so comfortable. Distinguish also from the contractions for they are—they're—and there are—there're—generally not acceptable in formal academic writing.

To, too: To introduces a prepositional phrase—to the lighthouse—or an infinitive form of the verb—to sail to the lighthouse. Too is an adverb that intensifies another adverb—it is not too far—or that means also—take me, too.

Toward, towards: Interchangeable, though American English favours the without-the-s version. In my dreams she comes toward (or towards) me.

Uninterested, disinterested: Uninterested means apathetic, as distinct from disinterested meaning impartial. A disinterested line judge favours neither player; an uninterested one misses many calls.

Wise: Considered a solecism when added to a noun to form an adverb: travelwise, computerwise, experiencewise.

Tutorial

Progress questions

Underline the correct word in parentheses in each sentence.

1. Darwin's *The Origin of the Species* (effected, affected) a profound change in theories of evolution.
2. In the wake of the scandal, Father Perowne lost his (moral, morale) authority and the moral of his congregation suffered.
3. A number of valuable pieces of jewellery (were, was) missing; the exact number of watches stolen (was, were) not known.
4. Beckham (past, passed) the ball to Rooney.
5. Everyone in the family was invited to her wedding (accept, except) Frank.
6. There is a friendly rivalry (between, among) teammates to see who will score first on a corner kick.
7. The lake he thought he saw in the distance was actually an (allusion, illusion) caused by the angle of the sun on the sand.
8. When she (eluded, alluded) to a policy Stalin promoted, the audience went silent.
9. His speech (affected, effected) the vote, but not in the way he intended.
10. The MLA has changed the protocols for (citing, siting) information taken from a government (webcite, website).
11. Political correctness, she argued, is a subtle form of (censorship, censureship).
12. He forgot to (bring, take) his dishes back to the kitchen.
13. For three days, Angela could barely (breath, breathe) because the air was so hot and smoggy.
14. They (assured, ensured) us that the policy would not go into (affect, effect) for another month.
15. Queen Ann, Pope wrote, sometimes took (council, counsel) and sometimes took tea.
16. Stars shine (continuously, continually) even though they are invisible during daylight hours.
17. Claudius has a guilty (conscious, conscience) but he cannot pray for forgiveness.

18. A burgundy (compliments, complements) roast beef but not pizza.
19. The denim used to make the first blue jeans was (course, coarse).
20. The letter (implied, inferred) that Jefferson lied, so Jefferson challenged his nemesis to a duel.
21. He was tried for treason, convicted, and (hanged, hung).
22. There are (fewer, less) flights out of Heathrow to South America.
23. Victorian servants working in country manor houses had to be (discreet, discrete).
24. The main (criteria, criterion) is experience, not education.
25. We (past, passed) a house the tour guide claimed was haunted.
26. His father refused to (lend, loan) him the money he needed to save the business.
27. He prayed fervently but still he was (lead, led) into temptation.
28. (Its, It's) in poor condition, firing on only three of (its, it's) cylinders.
29. Clark was too (ingenuous, ingenious) to believe that the porter might short change him.
30. I needed an hour on the (stationery, stationary) bicycle, followed by an hour of weight training.
31. Entropy was our (principle, principal) concern.
32. Ironically, he was (prejudice, prejudiced) against the French.
33. A small (per cent, percentage) of heavy smokers avoid serious illness.
34. It is a dangerous (procedure, precedure), but his hearing will be restored if it is successful.
35. My employer is (averse, adverse) to change.

Practical assignment

Compose a sentence that uses these words correctly:

whom
phenomena
morale

literally
averse
advise
already
among
lay
disinterested

Discussion points

Homonyms are words that have the same sound but different meaning: tail, tale; won, one; flea, flee; allude, elude; stationery, stationary; they're, their, there. How can you avoid confusing homonyms and using the wrong one in your writing?

Study and revision tip

Note that your grammar and spell checks will often miss errors in usage, so it is important, when you proofread your work, to check those words that often cause a usage error.

Answers to the progress questions

1. Darwin's *The Origin of the Species* (effected, affected) a profound change in theories of evolution.
2. In the wake of the scandal, Father Perowne lost his (moral, morale) authority and the moral of his congregation suffered.
3. A number of valuable pieces of jewellery (were, was) missing; the exact number of watches stolen (was, were) not known.
4. Beckham (past, passed) the ball to Rooney.
5. Everyone in the family was invited to her wedding (accept, except) Frank.
6. There is a friendly rivalry (between, among) teammates to see who will score first on a corner kick.
7. The lake he thought he saw in the distance was actually an (allusion, illusion) caused by the angle of the sun on the sand.
8. When she (eluded, alluded) to a policy Stalin promoted, the audience went silent.
9. His speech (affected, effected) the vote, but not in the way he intended.

10. The MLA has changed the protocols for (citing, siting) information taken from a government (webcite, website).
11. Political correctness, she argued, is a subtle form of (censorship, censureship).
12. He forgot to (bring, take) his dishes back to the kitchen.
13. For three days, Angela could barely (breath, breathe) because the air was so hot and smoggy.
14. They (assured, ensured) us that the policy would not go into (affect, effect) for another month.
15. Queen Ann, Pope wrote, sometimes took (council, counsel) and sometimes took tea.
16. Stars shine (continuously, continually) even though they are invisible during daylight hours.
17. Claudius has a guilty (conscious, conscience) but he cannot pray for forgiveness.
18. A burgundy (compliments, complements) roast beef but not pizza.
19. The denim used to make the first blue jeans was (course, coarse).
20. The letter (implied, inferred) that Jefferson lied, so Jefferson challenged his nemesis to a duel.
21. He was tried for treason, convicted, and (hanged, hung).
22. There are (fewer, less) flights out of Heathrow to South America.
23. Victorian servants working in country manor houses had to be (discreet, discrete).
24. The main (criteria, criterion) is experience, not education.
25. We (past, passed) a house the tour guide claimed was haunted.
26. His father refused to (lend, loan) him the money he needed to save the business.
27. He prayed fervently but still he was (lead, led) into temptation.
28. (Its, It's) in poor condition, firing on only three of (its, it's) cylinders.
29. Clark was too (ingenuous, ingenious) to believe that the porter might short change him.
30. I needed an hour on the (stationery, stationary) bicycle, followed by an hour of weight training.

31. Entropy was our (principle, <u>principal</u>) concern.
32. Ironically, he was (prejudice, <u>prejudiced</u>) against the French.
33. A small (per cent, <u>percentage</u>) of heavy smokers avoid serious illness.
34. It is a dangerous (<u>procedure</u>, precedure), but his hearing will be restored if it is successful.
35. My employer is (<u>averse</u>, adverse) to change.

Supplementary exercise A

Identify the errors in grammar and usage in the following sentences. Then revise the sentence to correct the errors.

1. Painted in 1956, Francis Bacon's *Study for Portrait II* sold at auction for fourteen million pounds, a record price for his work, in February, 2007.
2. Only a decade before he painted it, an art charity struggled to find buyers for any of Bacon's work.
3. A spirit of sorrow and dejection pervade Bacon's portrait, which might have emanated from his own despair over the end of his passionate relationship with fellow-artist Peter Lacy.
4. On Valentine's Day, many young men treat their girlfriends to a dozen roses, a box of rich chocolates and take them for a nice meal at an expensive restaurant.
5. One marriage counsellor claimed he had for clients a couple who broke up because the husband refused to share his popcorn with his wife. When they went to a movie.
6. Ballroom dancers have become famous and there are television programmes that feature celebrities competing against other celebrities to see who is the best at it.
7. Professional athletes make too much money now, no football player is worth fifteen million pounds a year.
8. Lord Hervey attended the London School of Economics. Though he did not stay long enough to earn a degree.
9. The dean of the College of Business was a professor of business management, but she fails to practice what she used to preach. Judging, at least, from the way she treats her staff.

10. Competition is so fierce now that any businessperson who does not have their own laptop and business software and Blackberry will find themselves at a disadvantage.
11. Sir Lionel has been diagnosed with Hepatitis C, and his doctors say either unprotected sex or a blood transfusion were the cause.
12. The paparazzi is refusing to take any photographs at the premiere because two of the stars of the film have lobbied for laws that they claim would limit their constitutional rights.
13. No vaccine exists to prevent Hepatitis C infection, however there are treatments available that are effective in more than half the cases.
14. The Health Protection Agency estimates that over 200,000 adults in England are infected with Hepatitis C, the majority of whom has not been diagnosed.
15. The first Body Shop opened in Brighton in 1976, now there are more than 2,000 stores around the world. Selling a range of skincare products.
16. Before Charlotte Church was a chat show host; she was an opera singer and even a pop star.
17. He found a stamp worth several thousand dollars to collectors on a letter his great-grandfather sent to his great-grandmother before he proposed marriage to her.
18. The study concluded that young adults with a college education were less likely to abuse drugs and alcohol than were young adults who never attended college, but if I was a college student today, I would question these findings.
19. If an actor wants to be nominated for an academy award, they should portray world leaders, athletes, or famous entertainers, recently actors portraying Queen Elizabeth II, Idi Amin, Ray Charles, Johnny Cash, Truman Capote, and Muhammad Ali have all been nominated.
20. Lists of the ten best English novels of all time will vary, but they will all have some entries in common. For example, at least one book by Charles Dickens and Jane Austen.

21. The Labour Party will have a new leader soon. Likely, before the end of the year.
22. It remains one of his most famous cartoons, and it depicted a group of dinosaurs smoking above the caption that read: 'the real reason the dinosaurs went extinct'.
23. Gilbert and Sullivan were feuding when they wrote *The Mikado*, but it became their most popular light opera, it had one of the longest runs of any of their works, and a lot of money was made from it for the D'Oly Carte Company.
24. The first meeting of the League of European Socialist Leaders were raided by the local police, with the support of the army.
25. The Texas senate were voting on a bill that would recommend harsher punishment for citizens hiring illegal immigrants from Mexico.
26. When he was a young boy, a blacking factory hired Charles Dickens to dye shoes, it was grinding work and he hated it.
27. If you are in a foreign country and you lose your visa or your passport, you need to go to that country's closest embassy or consulate office immediately and apply for a new one or you need to find an embassy or consulate office of your own country and apply for a new one.
28. Anyone who wants chips with their pizza are required to bring a permission slip from home.
29. The rapid melting of the glaciers indicate that global warming is accelerating.
30. School boards in some counties in some American states insist teachers include lessons on the biblical account of creationism in science class. Sometimes along side, sometimes in place of lessons in the theory of evolution.
31. If the Chancellor of the Exchequer had wrote the bill, the press will have been much more critical.
32. Eloisa and Abelard continued to correspond after she was cloistered in a convent and he in a monastery, but their letters burn with sorrow and despair because they

were ordered to physically and for the rest of their lives remain apart.

33. The British think Americans have no idea how to serve hot tea, Americans think the British have no idea how to serve ice tea.
34. The MP from Victoria wanted to introduce a bill that would make it illegal for babies to cry on airplanes, but other politicians in her party convinced her she would be the laughing stock of the country if she did so, after much cajoling.
35. Gym owners in Sweden reports that 80% of their customers who purchase memberships rarely exercise on a regular basis.
36. An Italian designer even makes suits to repel the rain, coated with Teflon.
37. Manufactures of packaged food must list the ingredients of their product. To prevent lawsuits from consumers with food allergies.
38. Applicants are not required to wear a suit, but they must be neatly dressed and good grooming should be paid attention to as well.
39. The Stratford Group of dieticians recommend serving vegetable juice instead of fruit juice, because fruit juice contains too much sugar, even for breakfast.
40. In any department store, customers can find a variety of salves, creams, ointments, unguents, lotions, and tonics for chapped lips, tired and puffy eyes, sagging skin, and wrinkled necks, at the cosmetics counter.
41. The words denim and jeans probably derive from the names of the cities, Nimes and Genoa, where the fabric that is used for making jeans were first wove.
42. My mother was a parishioner at St. Luke's for forty years, she felt it was her right and duty to tell the bishop exactly what she thought of the changes to the liturgy.
43. The next Archbishop of Canterbury can count on the support of most of his African bishops, if he opposes homosexual marriage.
44. As a rule, genius does not necessarily run in families, but it is true that some British families produced more than

one prominent writer, artist, or intellectual. Including the Rossettis, the Huxleys, and the Sackville-Wests.

45. Biographers have trouble accounting for the last years of Richard Lovelace's life, but he gave away his land and money in support of the Royalists. So he likely died in relative poverty and obscurity.
46. Professor Hilyard's analysis of police reports from London precincts do not support the widely-held belief that aberrant behaviour is more common when the moon is full.
47. If we share, and if the cost of the book is split between Ellen and I, we will both save £45.
48. If it wasn't for the lake effect snow off Lake Michigan, we would land on time.
49. Someone has parked their car in a space reserved for the handicapped without a sticker on it.
50. I don't know if the sophisticated lyrics or the haunting melody are going to linger longer in my memory.
51. The terrorists had released from captivity unharmed the Canadian journalist who was captured in the Christian sector of Kabul on February 10.
52. The Canadian journalist, who reports for the CBC, has not been released yet.
53. The BBC is reporting that these journalists have been captured, Mike Smith, who reports for the *New Jersey Dispatch*, Elaine Pater senior foreign correspondent for the *Washington World News*, Eric Moss a television reporter for Channel 9 in London, and Susan Pace a freelance writer on assignment with *Foreign Affairs Monthly*.
54. Dr. McPherson claims that the main problem with vegans are that they do not get enough protein in their diet.
55. At the end of Act I, it is revealed by the ghost of Hamlet's father that he was not killed by a snakebite, as the people of Denmark have been lead to believe, but by poison, poured into his ear by his own brother Claudius.
56. Eating disorders among models has become a concern of the entire fashion industry.

57. Flying over the Strait of Juan de Fuca, the San Juan Islands shimmer below in all of their pristine beauty.
58. A silk scarf is too fancy and wool scarf can itch, we each chose a cashmere scarf, a black one for my fiancé and a scarlet one for I.
59. Our budget for office supplies is depleted Marge had to order an expensive paper punch for Eliot, a new printer for Jane who accidentally pushed her last one off her desk and a box of fine linen paper for Louise who thinks a manager even a regional manager has to make a special impression on clients.
60. The flag of Japan consists of a red circle on a white background. To symbolise Japan's status as the land of the rising sun.
61. The Canadian flag consists of a red maple leaf on a white background that has red stripes at each end, the maple leaf represents Canada's status as a leading producer of maple syrup, the stripes symbolise the fact that the country stretches from the Atlantic to the Pacific.
62. The American flag, along with the British ensign, are in full view of passengers who land at the Baghdad airport.
63. The maximum jail time are three years, but only repeat offenders risks jail time.
64. The government has pro-rogued for the time being, the press are taking a holiday.
65. The Iranian government claimed that the British sailors and marines entered Iranian waters, displayed hostile intent, and that they were abusing in their attitude towards the Iranian sailors who arrested them.
66. One young British sailor issued a public apology, claiming that her and the other sailors and marines did enter Iranian waters but were being treated well by their captors. Though body language experts who viewed the video concluded that her words were not sincere.
67. Other than his three novels, *The Portrait of the Artist as a Young Man, Ulysses, and Finnegan's Wake* and one

collection of short stories, *Dubliners*, James Joyce did not write very much, but his work had an enormous impact on literature and literary criticism and changes the way novels are written and read.

68. My mother made the mistake of serving tea to the women in her church group in Styrofoam cups.
69. Heading south, the landscape began to change and we grew more confident that our holiday would be in beautiful country after all.
70. The company president was adverse to Daphne's proposal, arguing that it would have an averse effect on the sales of new parts.
71. Daphne countered that if her proposal was implemented, it would have a beneficial affect on the sale of laptops. Which has always been more profitable for the company.
72. The orchestra were already to begin but the conductor had not yet arrived because a terror alert stopped all trains leaving Victoria Station.
73. The manager admitted the dresses were overpriced and claimed she felt badly about the mistake but as of Thursday she has still not lowered the price.
74. If you have taken information from a web cite, you must site the source accurately.
75. At the Pig and Whistle now, there are less items on the menu but the quality of the food, especially the sandwiches, have improved.
76. The captured sailors and marines were criticised for confessing that they had strayed into Iranian waters, but they were subjected to periods of solitary confinement, their lives were at risk through veiled threats, and psychological intimidation.
77. The mother ship, a frigate, harboured a helicopter called a Lynx helicopter, which was to provide air cover and earlier had earlier provided air cover, but by the time the attack took place, it had returned to the frigate.
78. Foxrite is a small British company, but it is taking the risk of establishing a branch office in Los Angeles. Because many British citizens who work in the film

and television industry bought second homes in Los Angeles.

79. Baseball players and cricketers hit a ball with a bat, score runs, and if an opposing player catches a fly ball they have hit they are out, but, otherwise, the two sports are not similar.
80. After competing in the Olympic Games, the jet bringing the team home skidded off the runway, fortunately no one was injured.
81. Tea is rich in tannins, naturally occurring flavonoids, rich in antioxidants that may inhibit the growth of cancer cells, and cardiovascular health can also be improved by drinking tea.
82. Research suggests that black and green tea have comparable health benefits and that adding milk or cream to tea do not inhibit the body's ability to absorb tea's antioxidants.
83. Since the Samurai refused to engage in guerilla warfare or political assassination, the daimyo sometimes hired gangs of mercenaries called ninja, who was adept at night raids, espionage, and assassination.
84. The weather conditions at the Masters in Augusta was so severe this year that even the eventual winner was one shot over par. Which has not happened since 1952.
85. His company claims that within a few years we will be able to wear our mobile phones on our wrist, the way we wore a watch now, and that the numbers we want to call will be voice activated, so we will not have to carry around a special tool to depress the phone's tiny numbers, contrary to the rumours from competitors.
86. The examination was online, but since the server was down on Tuesday north of Stratford, half of the class could not write the exam, and the professor had to make up a new exam to prevent any security breaches and schedule a new time.
87. Explaining why it was so easy to allude security at Heathrow, he surprised the court by eluding to a passage from the Koran.

88. When he told them that he has been transferred, Harold's teenage children were not happy because they did not want to live so far way from their friends, but within a month they are swearing they will never leave this real beautiful island of Aruba.
89. So many students were openly smoking marijuana that the police ignored them, devoting their energy to breaking up fights and controlling the crowd instead. Which surged forward every time a new act came on stage.
90. Lady Jane Grey was Queen for nine days when she was just fifteen years old, the shortest reign and one of the youngest of any English monarch, the rightful heir, Henry VIII's daughter Mary hoped to spare her life but, under pressure from her Catholic advisors, she ordered Jane's execution.
91. When he was a young king, Henry VIII hunted avidly and jousted even with his knights, but by the time he was fifty, he slows down, as he grew fat and became despondent over his inability to father a son with any of his six wives.
92. They had four strong and tall sons, but only the one, who is just under six feet tall, won a basketball scholarship to a California college.
93. The number of Asians immigrating to the UK are beginning to decline.
94. Judging by her ingenious smile, she did not understand the off-colour joke the conductor told her.
95. Since there were no other sightings of the Loch Ness Monster last summer, I must imply that the young boy who swears he saw Nessie in August has a vivid imagination.
96. If they loose the game today, they will not advance to the next round.
97. Eighty-five percentage of eligible voters participated in the election for the President of France; the per cent of voter turnout is much lower in the United States.
98. The security guard felt badly about her use of excessive force, but the inquiry cleared her.

99. Two mosques in Liverpool were under surveillance because the Imams were known to be sympathetic to the al-Qaeda, the militant Islamic terrorist organization devoted to eliminating foreign influence in Muslim countries, the eradication of British and American infidels, and they have also vowed to destroy the state of Israel.
100. Comprised of a world-wide network of semi-autonomous cells, the American military cannot accurately assess the size of al-Qaeda or determine exactly who its leaders are.

Supplementary exercise B

Identify the errors in grammar and usage in the following sentences. Then revise the sentence to correct the errors.

1. A chlorofluorocarbon is one of a group of industrial chemicals that can damage the Earth's ozone layer, so named because it contains chlorine, fluorine, and carbon.
2. Ocean tides ebb and flow because the water is attracted by the gravitational pull of the sun and, especially, the moon. Which is smaller but much closer to the earth.
3. El Nino is an exceptionally strong warm current that brings heavy rains to the west coast of the United States.
4. UV is an abbreviation for Ultraviolet, the UV Index, a number that ranges from zero to ten, is a measure of the intensity of UV radiation.
5. If the UV index is above six, it is recommended by dermatologists that fair-skinned people avoid exposure to the sun. Due to an increased risk of skin cancer.
6. Lightening occurs when negatively charged ice crystals in the lower part of a storm cloud reacts with positively charged objects on the ground.
7. Lightening generates so much heat that the surrounding air expands rapidly, it explodes into the sound we know as thunder.
8. In June, 2000, an overloaded ferry capsized off the coast of Indonesia, killing over 500, in May, 2002, more than 370 people were drowned when a Bangladesh ferry sank, and, in September of the same year, an overloaded Senegalese ferry capsized, killing almost 2000 people.
9. He has been taking anti-psychotic drugs to treat schizophrenia for only a week before he stopped, because the side effects were worse than the delusions.

10. Iran and North Korea are building nuclear reactors. Despite opposition from the International Atomic Energy Agency.
11. The first number of a blood pressure reading measures the systolic pressure, which represents the amount of pressure in the blood vessels when the heart beats and pushes blood through the body. While the second number measures diastolic pressure, which represents the pressure in the blood vessels between beats, when the heart is resting.
12. Americans will never win the World Cup because they call football soccer. Which proves they think the game is more about power than finesse.
13. An enzyme is a protein in the body that promotes a particular chemical reaction.
14. Insurgents who oppose the U.S. presence and who hope to undermine the local government is responsible for the attack.
15. Hyundai's SUV has less cup holders than Toyota's.
16. Alice was conducting a study on the affect of gamma rays on tulip bulbs.
17. In the Summer Olympics more than 10,000 athletes, representing more than 200 countries, competes in more than 300 events.
18. In 1769, the coast of New Zealand was explored by Captain James Cook.
19. For seven straight years, one of the most amazing accomplishments in modern athletics was when Lance Armstrong won the Tour de France.
20. Four army captains and one marine colonel is representing the American military.
21. Among the victims was a dozen children.
22. Either France or Holland are going to represent the European Union at the summit.
23. France, along with Holland, are rejecting the constitution of the European Union.
24. A catastrophic tsunami killed over 200,000 people in Indonesia and eleven other countries bordering the Indian Ocean, in 2004.

25. If he has been convicted of fraud, he would have spent up to twenty-five years in prison.
26. After they were married, rice and rose petals covered the heads of the happy young couple.
27. As rugby players, women are not as good as men, but they are just as adept as auto racers, jockeys, and in playing golf.
28. A constant, whining sound kept us awake half the night.
29. Only one of the players have tested positive for steroids, but the whole team has been disqualified.
30. The Kyoto Protocol has been criticised because the restrictions on the use of fossil fuels are more stringent for developed than for developing countries under its terms.
31. While driving, mobile phones should not be used.
32. Many retired people, who we know, stay active by working as volunteers for various social agencies.
33. For her encore she sung 'Love is a Rose'.
34. She is so passionate about cleaning up Rainbow Park she has even wrote to the Queen to enlist her support.
35. There is an unwritten agreement among former Prime Ministers that they will be circumspect when the press ask them to assess the policies of the current Prime Minister.
36. Most conspiracy theorists assert that the government, the military, organised religion, and big corporations regularly deceive the public on a frequent basis.
37. The taxes in America are not as high as most European nations, but Americans do not have as many government funded social programs.
38. In the 1960's, auto makers did not highlight their vehicles safety features in their marketing campaigns, today they do.
39. The day after a new President is elected in America, ambitious politicians begin to campaign to replace him.
40. Palestinian refugee camps in Lebanon has been breeding grounds for Islamic terrorists, in part because conditions in these camps are wretched.

41. At one time, matchmakers, were, stereotypically, meddling old women, but now sophisticated computer programs help lonely hearts find there perfect mate.
42. Even inmates, who have committed heinous crimes, get mail from women and men expressing an interest in meeting them.
43. Labour unions are less likely to strike today than they were in the passed because their and management's negotiating skills are considerably more sophisticated.
44. If Elsie comes with Wilson and I, there will be enough room in Martin's car to take both he and his grandmother.
45. Televised debates are an affective method of assessing the competence of political candidates.
46. Like the bow tie, the Windsor knot is somewhat out of fashion now among those who wear a necktie because they think their face looks fat if they wear one.
47. My Uncle loves to go fly fishing in the summer, ice fishing in the winter, and when he is on holiday, he loves to go deep sea fishing.
48. Professional shoe shiners will sometimes heat the shoe leather with an open flame, which opens up the pores of the leather and helps them apply to them a deep, glossy shine.
49. Films that are full of dazzling special effects, that cast famous movie stars, and in which endless action is present usually make a lot of money.
50. Cannes is a suburb of Nice, famous for its glamorous film festival held each May.
51. Many large cities host film festivals, none are more star-studded and spectacular than Cannes.
52. The father of the bride was a widower and the mother of the groom was a widow, they married exactly one year after their children's wedding.
53. Orange juice is a good source of vitamin C, but when it is sweetened with corn syrup which is high in fructose, it's nutritional benefits are diminished.
54. Aerospace scientists scoffed at futurists who predicted we would all fly to work, using our own individual jet pack because they knew that even if the technology

could be perfected, it would be an extremely dangerous mode of transport.

55. I don't know if we would call Marna an addict, but she does go shopping everyday.
56. A petrol station manager cannot set their own petrol prices, they must charge what the oil companies prescribe.
57. The invitation is for both my wife and I, but she is away on business that day.
58. He was so determined to get rich quick, he was willing even to bend, if not break, the law.
59. She amended her will, irrregardless of the problems she knew it would cause.
60. If convicted, jail time for the defendant could be as much as twenty-five years.
61. The rule does not seem to be applying to anyone but I.
62. She was almost as worried about the consequences of the new legislation as me.
63. In this country, the typical jury deliberates for three days before finally delivering their verdict.
64. He claimed he read the Bible every day but it was apparent that he was being ingenuous when he did not know its first book is Genesis.
65. If a patient suffering from bipolar disorder does not respond to therapy, they can take medication.
66. On Trial Island, clearly visible from Beach Drive, is clusters of tall, yellow daffodils.
67. Planning a surprise party and keeping it secret is impossible if the birthday girl has young children.
68. No new bowlers for the team has been recruited, but we still expect a winning season.
69. Vilified as a radical Marxist early in his career, most people now regard the Minister of Defence as a moderate.
70. If you drink several bottles of sparkling water each day is another way to lose weight.
71. Exhausted by three hours of overtime, most players returned to their room, laid down on their beds, and promptly fell asleep.
72. Her letters or her journal are going up for auction to raise money for the museum.

73. For we accountants, holiday season begins in May.
74. Inside the vault, hidden in the recess of the back wall was gold coins worth a small fortune.
75. It will have a profound affect on the income of people of retirement age, but it will not effect younger citizens.
76. His television set, along with all of his stereo equipment, were stolen.
77. The last time we were altogether was at my uncle's funeral.
78. The general public was adverse to the ads, which most people felt were in poor taste.
79. My brother is eight years younger than me, but he already has four children.
80. The accident left him with a nasty, little scar, above and below his right eye.
81. Flight attendants served first-class passengers a complementary glass of champagne.
82. Naturally, the cup, filled with hot tea, was the one that crashed to the floor.
83. The American delegation returned continuously to arguments about fairness, whenever the talk turned to exceptions to the accord for developing nations.
84. She never has and never will condone rudeness from her children.
85. As of today, there has been no farther word on the fate of the hostages.
86. In our university library, there are less books about reincarnation than I thought there would be.
87. We objected to his singing 'God Save the Queen' because he is from South Africa.
88. The runner with the fastest time will get their picture on the front page of the local newspaper.
89. It was an impracticable solution, one that would likely exacerbate the problem not solve it.
90. Nearly all the reviewers criticised it's plot, which was impossible to follow.
91. For three days after her surgery, Blossom just laid on her blanket and refused to eat.
92. She was nearly eighty, but she lead an expedition to the Arctic to study the health of the polar bear population

to help the government determine weather or not to put the polar bear on the endangered species list.

93. Like you have told me many times, honesty is the best policy.
94. Finally off her diet, she literally devoured those fish and chips with her eyes.
95. As an evangelist, he claimed he lead his life based upon sound moral principals.
96. The war is not going well, but the moral of the troops remains high.
97. Neither the Prime Minister nor the Chancellor of the Exchequer have been implicated in the scandal.
98. Having bitten yet another child, the police officer had no choice but to shoot the pit bull dead.
99. Her aquiline nose is one of her features that are particularly striking.
100. He made arrangements to rent a small Volkswagen because he thought it would be the least expensive, he was shocked when he learned how much it costs to rent even a modest car.

Answers to supplementary exercise A

Identify the errors in grammar and usage in the following sentences. Then revise the sentence to correct the errors.

1. A misplaced modifier. Change to: Painted in 1956, Francis Bacon's *Study for Portrait II* sold at auction in February, 2007 for fourteen million pounds, a record price for his work.
2. A dangling modifier. Change to: Only a decade before he painted *Study for Portrait II*, Bacon struggled, even with the help of an art charity to find buyers for any of his work.
3. Subject-verb agreement error. Change to: A spirit of sorrow and dejection pervades Bacon's portrait, which might have emanated from his own despair over the end of his passionate relationship with fellow-artist Peter Lacy.
4. Faulty parallelism. Change to: On Valentine's Day, many young men treat their girlfriends to a dozen roses, a box of rich chocolates, and a nice meal at an expensive restaurant.
5. Sentence Fragment. Change to: One marriage counsellor claimed he had for clients a couple who broke up because the husband refused to share his popcorn with his wife, when they went to a movie.
6. Ambiguous pronoun. Change to: Ballroom dancers have become famous and there are television programmes that feature celebrities competing against other celebrities to see who is the best ballroom dancer.

7. Run-on sentence. Change to: Professional athletes make too much money now; no football player is worth fifteen million pounds a year.
8. Sentence fragment. Change to: Lord Hervey attended the London School of Economics, though he did not stay long enough to earn a degree.
9. Sentence fragment. Change to: The dean of the College of Business was a professor of business management, but she fails to practice what she used to preach, judging, at least, from the way she treats her staff.
10. Faulty pronoun agreement. Change to: Competition is so fierce now that any businessperson who does not have his or her own laptop, with business software and Blackberry will find him or herself at a disadvantage.
11. Error in subject-verb agreement. Change to: Sir Lionel has been diagnosed with Hepatitis C, and his doctors say either unprotected sex or a blood transfusion was the cause.
12. Ambiguous pronoun reference. Change to: The paparazzi is (are also correct) refusing to take any photographs at the premiere because two of the stars of the film have lobbied for laws that the paparazzi claim would limit their constitutional rights.
13. Run-on sentence. Change to: No vaccine exists to prevent Hepatitis C infection; however there are treatments available that are effective in more than half the cases.
14. Misplaced modifier. Change to: The Health Protection Agency estimates that over 200,000 adults in England, the majority of whom has (have also correct, maybe better because preceded by 'the') not been diagnosed, are infected with Hepatitis C.
15. A run on sentence and a sentence fragment and a misplaced modifier. Change to: The first Body Shop opened in Brighton in 1976. Now there are more than 2,000 stores, selling a range of beauty products, around the world.
16. Error in punctuation. Change to: Before Charlotte Church was a chat show host, she was an opera singer and even a pop star.

17. Misplaced modifier. Change to: He found on a letter his great-grandfather sent to his great grandmother before he proposed marriage to her, a stamp worth several thousand dollars to collectors.
18. Error in verb tense; subjunctive needed. Change to: The study concluded that young adults with a college education were less likely to abuse drugs and alcohol than were young adults who never attended college, but if I were a college student today, I would question these findings.
19. Pronoun agreement error and a run-on sentence. Change to: If actors want to be nominated for an academy award, they should portray world leaders, athletes, or famous entertainers. Recently actors portraying Queen Elizabeth II, Idi Amin, Ray Charles, Johnny Cash, Truman Capote, and Muhammad Ali have all been nominated.
20. Sentence fragment. Change to: Lists of the ten best English novels of all time will vary, but they will all have some entries in common. For example, at least one book by Charles Dickens and Jane Austen will be on the list.
21. Sentence fragment. Change to: The Labour Party will have a new leader soon, likely, before the end of the year.
22. Error in verb tense. Change to: It remains one of his most famous cartoons, and it depicts a group of dinosaurs smoking above the caption that read: 'the real reason the dinosaurs went extinct'.
23. Faulty parallelism. Change to: Gilbert and Sullivan were feuding when they wrote *The Mikado*, but it became their most popular light opera, it had one of the longest runs of any of their works, and it made a lot of money for the D'Oly Carte Company.
24. Error in subject-verb agreement. Change to: The first meeting of the League of European Socialist Leaders was raided by the local police, with the support of the army.
25. Error in subject-verb agreement. Change to: The Texas senate was voting on a bill that would recommend harsher

punishment for citizens hiring illegal immigrants from Mexico.

26. A dangling modifier and a run-on sentence. Change to: When he was a young boy, Charles Dickens worked in a blacking factory, where he dyed shoes. It was grinding work and he hated it.
27. Ambiguous pronoun reference. Change to: If you are in a foreign country and you lose your visa or your passport, you need to go to that country's closest embassy or consulate office immediately and apply for a new visa or passport or you need to find an embassy or consulate office of your own country and apply for the new documents.
28. Error in subject-verb agreement. Change to: Anyone who wants chips with their (or his or her) pizza is required to bring a permission slip from home.
29. Error in subject-verb agreement. Change to: The rapid melting of the glaciers indicates that global warming is accelerating.
30. Sentence fragment. Change to: School boards in some counties in some American states insist teachers include lessons on the biblical account of creationism in science class, sometimes along side, sometimes in place of lessons in the theory of evolution.
31. Error in verb tense. Change to: If the Chancellor of the Exchequer had written the bill, the press would have been much more critical.
32. Split infinitive. Change to: Eloisa and Abelard continued to correspond after she was cloistered in a convent and he in a monastery, but their letters burn with sorrow and despair because they were ordered to live physically apart for the rest of their lives.
33. Run-on sentence. Change to: The British think Americans have no idea how to serve hot tea; (or ,while) Americans think the British have no idea how to serve ice tea.
34. Misplaced modifier. Change to: The MP from Victoria wanted to introduce a bill that would make it illegal for babies to cry on airplanes, but, after much cajoling,

other politicians in her party convinced her she would be the laughing stock of the country if she did so.

35. Error in subject-verb agreement. Change to: Gym owners in Sweden report that 80% of their customers who purchase memberships rarely exercise on a regular basis.
36. Misplaced modifier. Change to: An Italian designer even makes suits coated with Teflon to repel the rain.
37. Sentence fragment. Change to: Manufactures of packaged food must list the ingredients of their product, to prevent lawsuits from consumers with food allergies.
38. Faulty parallelism. Change to: Applicants are not required to wear a suit, but they must be neatly dressed and well groomed.
39. Misplaced modifier. Change to: The Stratford Group of dieticians recommend (or recommends) serving vegetable juice instead of fruit juice even for breakfast, because fruit juice contains too much sugar.
40. Misplaced modifiers. Change to: In any department store, customers can find, at the cosmetics counter, a variety of salves, creams, ointments, unguents, lotions, and tonics for chapped lips, tired and puffy eyes, sagging skin, and wrinkled necks,
41. Error in subject-verb agreement and verb tense. Change to: The words denim and jeans probably derive from the names of the cities, Nimes and Genoa, where the fabric that is used for making jeans was first woven.
42. Run-on sentence. Change to: My mother was a parishioner at St. Luke's for forty years, and she felt it was her right and duty to tell the bishop exactly what she thought of the changes to the liturgy.
43. Pronoun reference error. Change to: The next Archbishop of Canterbury can count on the support of most of his or her African bishops, if he or she opposes homosexual marriage.
44. Sentence fragment. Change to: As a rule, genius does not necessarily run in families, but it is true that some British families, Including the Rossettis, the Huxleys,

and the Sackville-Wests, produced more than one prominent writer, artist, or intellectual.

45. Sentence fragment. Change to: Biographers have trouble accounting for the last years of Richard Lovelace's life, but he gave away his land and money in support of the Royalists, so he likely died in relative poverty and obscurity.
46. Subject-verb agreement error. Change to: Professor Hilyard's analysis of police reports from London precincts does not support the widely-held belief that aberrant behaviour is more common when the moon is full.
47. Pronoun agreement error. Change to: If we share, and if the cost of the book is split between Ellen and me, we will both save £45.
48. Error in verb tense. Change to: If it weren't for the lake effect snow off Lake Michigan, we would land on time.
49. Misplaced modifier. Change to: Someone has parked their (or his or her) car, without a sticker on it, in a space reserved for the handicapped.
50. Subject-verb agreement error. Change to: I don't know if the sophisticated lyrics or the haunting melody is going to linger longer in my memory.
51. Verb tense error. Change to: The terrorists have released from captivity unharmed the Canadian journalist who was captured in the Christian sector of Kabul on February 10.
52. Comma error; the clause is restrictive. Change to: The Canadian journalist who reports for the CBC has not been released yet.
53. Punctuation errors. Change to: The BBC is reporting that these journalists have been captured: Mike Smith, who reports for the *New Jersey Dispatch*; Elaine Pater, senior foreign correspondent for the *Washington World News*; Eric Moss, a television reporter for Channel 9 in London; and Susan Pace a freelance writer on assignment with *Foreign Affairs Monthly*.
54. Subject-verb agreement error. Change to: Dr. McPherson claims that the main problem with vegans is that they do not get enough protein in their diet.

55. Dangling modifier, verb tense, and punctuation errors. Change to: At the end of Act I, the ghost of Hamlet's father reveals that he was not killed by a snakebite, as the people of Denmark had been lead to believe, but by poison, poured into his ear by his own brother, Claudius.
56. Error in subject-verb agreement. Change to: Eating disorders among models have become a concern of the entire fashion industry.
57. Dangling modifier. Change to: Flying over the Strait of Juan de Fuca, we saw the San Juan Islands shimmer below, in all of their pristine beauty.
58. A run on sentence and an error in pronoun case. Change to: A silk scarf is too fancy and wool scarf can itch, so we each chose a cashmere scarf, a black one for my fiancé and a scarlet one for me.
59. A run-on sentence and several punctuation errors. Change to: Our budget for office supplies is depleted. Marge had to order an expensive paper punch for Eliot; a new printer for Jane, who accidentally pushed her last one off her desk; and a box of fine linen paper for Louise, who thinks a manager, even a regional manager, has to make a special impression on clients.
60. A sentence fragment. Change to: The flag of Japan consists of a red circle on a white background to symbolise (or symbolizing) Japan's status as the land of the rising sun.
61. A run-on sentence. Change to: The Canadian flag consists of a red maple leaf on a white background that has red stripes at each end. The maple leaf represents Canada's status as a leading producer of maple syrup. The stripes symbolise the fact that the country stretches from the Atlantic to the Pacific.
62. Subject-verb agreement error. Change to: The American flag, along with the British ensign, is in full view of passengers who land at the Baghdad airport. (Note that 'are' would be fine if the two subjects were joined together by 'and').
63. Two subject-verb agreement errors. Change to: The maximum jail time is three years, but only repeat offenders risk jail time.

64. Run-on sentence. Change to: The government has pro-rogued for the time being, so the press are ('is' also acceptable) taking a holiday.
65. Faulty parallelism. Change to: The Iranian government claimed that the British sailors and marines entered Iranian waters, displayed hostile intent, and were abusive towards the Iranian sailors who arrested them.
66. Error in pronoun case and a sentence fragment. Change to: One young British sailor issued a public apology, claiming that she and the other sailors and marines did enter Iranian waters but were being treated well by their captors, though body language experts who viewed the video concluded that her words were not sincere.
67. Verb tense error. Change to: Other than his three novels, *The Portrait of the Artist as a Young Man, Ulysses, and Finnegan's Wake,* and one collection of short stories, *Dubliners*, James Joyce did not write very much, but his work had an enormous impact on literature and literary criticism and changed the way novels are written and read.
68. A misplaced modifier. Change to: My mother made the mistake of serving tea in Styrofoam cups to the women in her church group.
69. Dangling modifier. Change to: Heading south, we noticed that the landscape began to change, and we grew more confident that our holiday would be in beautiful country after all.
70. Usage errors. Change to: The company president was averse to Daphne's proposal, arguing that it would have an adverse affect on the sales of new parts.
71. Error in subject-verb agreement and usage and a sentence fragment. Change to: Daphne countered that if her proposal were implemented, it would have a beneficial effect on the sale of laptops, which has always been more profitable for the company.
72. Punctuation, usage, and verb tense errors. Change to: The orchestra were ('was' also fine) all ready begin, but the conductor had not yet arrived because a terror alert had stopped all trains leaving Victoria Station.

73. Usage and punctuation error. Change to: The manager admitted the dresses were overpriced and claimed she felt bad about the mistake, but as of Thursday she has still not lowered the price.
74. Usage error. Change to: If you have taken information from a website, you must cite the source accurately.
75. Usage and subject-verb agreement errors. Change to: At the Pig and Whistle now, there are fewer items on the menu. but the quality of the food, especially the sandwiches, has improved.
76. Run-on sentence, verb tense error, and comma error. Change to: The captured sailors and marines were criticised for confessing that they had strayed into Iranian waters, but they had been subjected to periods of solitary confinement. Their lives were at risk through veiled threats and psychological intimidation.
77. Too wordy. Change to: The mother ship, a frigate, harbored a Lynx helicopter, which had earlier provided air cover, but by the time the attack took place, it had returned to the frigate.
78. Sentence fragment and verb tense error. Change to: Foxrite is a small British company, but it is taking the risk of establishing a branch office in Los Angeles, because many British citizens who work in the film and television industry have bought second homes in Los Angeles.
79. Too wordy because of faulty parallelism. Change to: Baseball players and cricketers hit a ball with a bat, score runs, and are called out if an opposing player catches a fly ball they have hit, but, otherwise, the two sports are not similar.
80. A dangling modifier and a run-on sentence. Change to: The jet bringing the team home after the team competed in the Olympic Games, skidded off the runway; fortunately no one was injured.
81. Faulty parallelism. Change to: Tea is rich in tannins, naturally occurring flavonoids, rich in antioxidants that may inhibit the growth of cancer cells, and improve cardiovascular health.

82. Verb tense error. Change to: Research suggests that black and green tea have comparable health benefits and that adding milk or cream to tea does not inhibit the body's ability to absorb tea's antioxidants.
83. Verb tense error. Change to: Since the Samurai refused to engage in guerilla warfare or political assassination, the daimyo sometimes hired gangs of mercenaries called ninja, who were adept at night raids, espionage, and assassination.
84. Verb tense error and sentence fragment. Change to: The weather conditions at the Masters in Augusta were so severe this year that even the eventual winner was one shot over par, which has not happened since 1952.
85. Verb tense error and misplaced modifier. Change to: His company claims that within a few years we will be able to wear our mobile phones on our wrist, the way we wear a watch now, and that the numbers we want to call will be voice activated, so contrary to the rumours from competitors, we will not have to carry around a special tool to depress the phone's tiny numbers.
86. Misplaced modifiers. Change to: The examination was online, but since on Tuesday the server was down north of Stratford, half of the class could not write the exam, and the professor had to schedule a new time and make up a new exam to prevent any security breaches.
87. Usage errors. Change to: Explaining why it was so easy to elude security at Heathrow, he surprised the court by alluding to a passage from the Koran.
88. Verb tense and usage errors. Change to: When he told them that he had been transferred, Harold's teenage children were not happy because they did not want to live so far way from their friends, but within a month they were swearing they will never leave this really beautiful island of Aruba.
89. Misplaced modifier and sentence fragment. Change to: So many students were openly smoking marijuana that the police ignored them, devoting their energy instead to breaking up fights and controlling the crowd, which surged forward every time a new act came on stage.

90. Run-on sentence, comma error, and coordination error. Change to: Lady Jane Grey was Queen for nine days when she was just fifteen years old, the shortest reign by one of the youngest of any English monarch. The rightful heir, Henry VIII's daughter Mary, hoped to spare her life but, under pressure from her Catholic advisors, she ordered Jane's execution.
91. Misplaced modifier, verb tense error, and comma error. Change to: When he was a young king, Henry VIII hunted avidly and even jousted with his knights, but by the time he was fifty, he slowed down, as he grew fat and became despondent over his inability to father a son, with any of his six wives.
92. Comma error. Change to: They had four strong and tall sons, but only the one who is just under six feet tall won a basketball scholarship to a California college.
93. Subject-verb agreement error. Change to: The number of Asians immigrating to the UK is beginning to decline.
94. Usage error. Change to: Judging by her ingenuous smile, she did not understand the off-colour joke the conductor told her.
95. Usage error. Change to: Since there were no other sightings of the Loch Ness Monster last summer, I must infer that the young boy who swears he saw Nessie in August has a vivid imagination.
96. Usage error. Change to: If they lose the game today, they will not advance to the next round.
97. Usage error. Change to: Eighty-five per cent of eligible voters participated in the election for the President of France; the percentage of voter turnout is much lower in the United States.
98. Usage error. Change to: The security guard felt bad about her use of excessive force, but the inquiry cleared her.
99. Faulty parallelism. Change to: Two mosques in Liverpool were under surveillance because the Imams were known to be sympathetic to the al-Qaeda, the militant Islamic terrorist organization devoted to eliminating foreign influence in Muslim countries, the eradication

of British and American infidels, and the destruction of the state of Israel.

100. Dangling modifier. Change to: The American military cannot accurately assess the size of al-Qaeda or determine exactly who its leaders are, because the organization is comprised of a world-wide network of semi-autonomous cells.

Answers to supplementary exercise B

Identify the errors in grammar and usage in the following sentences. Then revise the sentence to correct the errors.

1. Misplaced modifier. Change to: A chlorofluorocarbon, so named because it contains chlorine, fluorine, and carbon, is one of a group of industrial chemicals that can damage the Earth's ozone layer.
2. Sentence fragment. Change to: Ocean tides ebb and flow because the water is attracted by the gravitational pull of the sun and, especially, the moon, which is smaller but much closer to the earth.
3. Comma error. Change to: El Nino is an exceptionally strong, warm current that brings heavy rains to the west coast of the United States.
4. Run-on sentence. Change to: UV is an abbreviation for Ultraviolet. The UV Index, a number that ranges from zero to ten, is a measure of the intensity of UV radiation.
5. Error in passive voice and a sentence fragment. Change to: If the UV index is above six, dermatologists recommend that fair-skinned people avoid exposure to the sun, due to an increased risk of skin cancer.
6. Subject-verb agreement error. Change to: Lightening occurs when negatively charged ice crystals in the lower part of a storm cloud react with positively charged objects on the ground.
7. Run-on sentence. Change to: Lightening generates so much heat that the surrounding air expands rapidly, exploding [or and explodes] into the sound we know as thunder.

8. Semi-colon error. Change to: In June, 2000, an overloaded ferry capsized off the coast of Indonesia, killing over 500; in May, 2002, more than 370 people were drowned when a Bangladesh ferry sank; and, in September of the same year, an overloaded Senegalese ferry capsized, killing almost 2000 people.
9. Verb tense error. Change to: He had been taking anti-psychotic drugs to treat schizophrenia for only a week before he stopped, because the side effects were worse than the delusions.
10. Sentence fragment. Change to: Iran and North Korea are building nuclear reactors, despite opposition from the International Atomic Energy Agency.
11. Sentence fragment. Change to: The first number of a blood pressure reading measures the systolic pressure, which represents the amount of pressure in the blood vessels when the heart beats and pushes blood through the body while the second number measures diastolic pressure, which represents the pressure in the blood vessels between beats, when the heart is resting.
12. Sentence fragment. Change to: Americans will never win the World Cup because they call football soccer, which proves they think the game is more about power than finesse.
13. Misplaced modifier. Change to: An enzyme is a protein that promotes a particular chemical reaction in the body.
14. Subject-verb agreement error. Change to: Insurgents who oppose the U.S. presence and who hope to undermine the local government are responsible for the attack.
15. Usage error. Change to: Hyundai's SUV has fewer cup holders than Toyota's.
16. Usage error. Change to: Alice was conducting a study on the effect of gamma rays on tulip bulbs.
17. Subject-verb agreement error. Change to: In the Summer Olympics more than 10,000 athletes, representing more than 200 countries, compete in more than 300 events.

18. Usage error. Change to: In 1769, Captain James Cook explored the coast of New Zealand.
19. Dangling modifier. Change to: For seven straight years, Lance Armstrong won the Tour de France, one of the most amazing accomplishments in modern athletics.
20. Subject-verb agreement error. Change to: Four army captains and one marine colonel are representing the American military.
21. Subject-verb agreement error. Change to: Among the victims were a dozen children.
22. Subject-verb agreement error. Change to: Either France or Holland is going to represent the European Union at the summit.
23. Subject-verb agreement error. Change to: France, along with Holland, is rejecting the constitution of the European Union.
24. Misplaced modifier. Change to: In 2004, a catastrophic tsunami killed over 200,000 people in Indonesia and eleven other countries bordering the Indian Ocean.
25. Verb tense error. Change to: If he had been convicted of fraud, he would have spent up to twenty-five years in prison.
26. Dangling modifier. Change to: After they were married, the happy young couple had their heads covered with rice and rose petals.
27. Faulty parallelism. Change to: As rugby players, women are not as good as men, but they are just as adept as auto racers, jockeys, and golfers.
28. Comma error. Change to: A constant whining sound kept us awake half the night.
29. Subject-verb agreement error. Change to: Only one of the players has tested positive for steroids, but the whole team has been disqualified.
30. Misplaced modifier. Change to: The Kyoto Protocol has been criticised because, under its terms, the restrictions on the use of fossil fuels are more stringent for developed than for developing countries.
31. Dangling modifier. Change to: Drivers should not use mobile phones.

32. Pronoun error. Change to: Many retired people, whom we know, stay active by working as volunteers for various social agencies.
33. Verb tense error. Change to: For her encore she sang 'Love is a Rose'.
34. Verb tense error. Change to: She is so passionate about cleaning up Rainbow Park she has even written to the Queen to enlist her support.
35. Subject-verb agreement error. Change to: There is an unwritten agreement among former Prime Ministers that they will be circumspect when the press asks them to assess the policies of the current Prime Minister.
36. Redundancy. Change to: Most conspiracy theorists assert that the government, the military, organised religion, and big corporations regularly deceive the public.
37. Faulty comparison. Change to: The taxes in America are not as high they are in most European nations, but Americans do not have as many government funded social programs.
38. Run-on sentence. Change to: In the 1960's, auto makers did not highlight their vehicles safety features in their marketing campaigns; today they do.
39. Sexist pronoun use. Change to: The day after a new President is elected in America, ambitious politicians begin to campaign to replace him or her.
40. Verb tense error. Change to: Palestinian refugee camps in Lebanon have been breeding grounds for Islamic terrorists, in part because conditions in these camps are wretched.
41. Usage error. Change to: At one time, matchmakers, were, stereotypically, meddling old women, but now sophisticated computer programs help lonely hearts find their perfect mate.
42. Comma error. Change to: Even inmates who have committed heinous crimes get mail from women and men expressing an interest in meeting them.
43. Usage error. Change to: Labour unions are less likely to strike today than they were in the past because their

and management's negotiating skills are considerably more sophisticated.

44. Pronoun case errors. Change to: If Elsie comes with Wilson and me, there will be enough room in Martin's car to take both him and his grandmother.
45. Usage error. Change to: Televised debates are an effective method of assessing the competence of political candidates.
46. Pronoun reference error. Change to: Like the bow tie, the Windsor knot is somewhat out of fashion now among those who wear a necktie because a Windsor knot can make a face look fat.
47. Faulty parallelism. Change to: My Uncle loves to go fly fishing in the summer, ice fishing in the winter, and deep sea fishing when he is on holiday.
48. Pronoun reference error. Change to: Professional shoe shiners will sometimes heat the shoe leather with an open flame, which opens up the pores of the leather and helps the shoe shiner apply a deep, glossy shine.
49. Faulty parallelism. Change to: Films that are full of dazzling special effects, that cast famous movie stars, and that feature endless action usually make a lot of money.
50. Misplaced modifier. Change to: Famous for it glamorous film festival held each May, Cannes is a suburb of Nice.
51. Run-on sentence and subject-verb agreement error. Change to: Many large cities host film festivals, but none is more star-studded and spectacular than Cannes.
52. Run-on sentence. Change to: The father of the bride was a widower and the mother of the groom was a widow. They married exactly one year after their children's wedding.
53. Usage error. Change to: Orange juice is a good source of vitamin C, but when it is sweetened with corn syrup which is high in fructose, its nutritional benefits are diminished.
54. Vague pronoun reference. Change to: Aerospace scientists scoffed at futurists who predicted we would all fly to work, using our own individual jet pack

because the scientists knew that even if the technology could be perfected, the jet pack would be an extremely dangerous mode of transport.

55. Usage error. Change to: I don't know if we would call Marna an addict, but she does go shopping every day.
56. Run-on sentence and pronoun agreement error. Change to: Petrol station managers cannot set their own petrol prices; they must charge what the oil companies prescribe.
57. Pronoun case error. Change to: The invitation is for both my wife and me, but she is away on business that day.
58. Usage error. Change to: He was so determined to get rich quickly, he was willing even to bend, if not break, the law.
59. Usage error. Change to: She amended her will, regardless of the problems she knew it would cause.
60. Dangling modifier. Change to: If convicted, the defendant could get as much as twenty-five years of jail time.
61. Pronoun case error. Change to: The rule does not seem to be applying to anyone but me.
62. Pronoun case error. Change to: She was almost as worried about the consequences of the new legislation as I [was.]
63. Pronoun agreement error. Change to: In this country, the typical jury deliberates for three days before finally delivering its verdict.
64. Usage error. Change to: He claimed he read the Bible every day, but it was apparent that he was being disingenuous when he did not know its first book is Genesis.
65. Pronoun agreement error. Change to: If a patient suffering from bipolar disorder does not respond to therapy, he or she can take medication.
66. Subject-verb agreement error. Change to: On Trial Island, clearly visible from Beach Drive, are clusters of tall, yellow daffodils.
67. Subject-verb agreement error. Change to: Planning a surprise party and keeping it secret are impossible if the birthday girl has young children.

68. Subject-verb agreement error. Change to: No new bowlers for the team have been recruited, but we still expect a winning season.
69. Dangling modifier. Change to: Vilified as a radical Marxist early in his career, the Minister of Defence is regarded now by most people as a moderate.
70. Subject-verb agreement error. Change to: Drinking several bottles of sparkling water each day is another way to lose weight.
71. Verb tense error. Change to: Exhausted by three hours of overtime, most players returned to their room, lay down on their beds, and promptly fell asleep.
72. Subject-verb agreement error. Change to: Her letters or her journal is going up for auction to raise money for the museum.
73. Pronoun case error. Change to: For us accountants, holiday season begins in May.
74. Subject-verb agreement error. Change to: Inside the vault, hidden in the recess of the back wall were gold coins worth a small fortune.
75. Usage errors. Change to: It will have a profound effect on the income of people of retirement age, but it will not affect younger citizens.
76. Subject-verb agreement error. Change to: His television set, along with all of his stereo equipment, was stolen.
77. Usage error. Change to: The last time we were all together was at my uncle's funeral.
78. Usage error. Change to: The general public was averse to the ads, which most people felt were in poor taste.
79. Pronoun case error. Change to: My brother is eight years younger than I [am], but he already has four children.
80. Comma error. Change to: The accident left him with a nasty little scar, above and below his right eye.
81. Usage error. Change to: Flight attendants served first-class passengers a complimentary glass of champagne.
82. Comma error. Change to: Naturally, the cup filled with hot tea was the one that crashed to the floor.
83. Usage error and misplaced modifier. Change to: The American delegation returned continually to arguments

about fairness, whenever the talk turned to exceptions for developing nations to the accord.

84. Verb tense error. Change to: She never has condoned and never will condone rudeness from her children.
85. Usage error. Change to: As of today, there has been no further word on the fate of the hostages.
86. Usage error. Change to: In our university library, there are fewer books about reincarnation than I thought there would be.
87. Pronoun case error. Change to: We objected to him singing 'God Save the Queen' because he is from South Africa.
88. Pronoun agreement error. Change to: The runner with the fastest time will get his or her picture on the front page of the local newspaper.
89. Usage error. Change to: It was an impractical solution, one that would likely exacerbate the problem not solve it.
90. Usage error. Change to: Nearly all the reviewers criticised its plot, which was impossible to follow.
91. Verb tense error. Change to: For three days after her surgery, Blossom just lay on her blanket and refused to eat.
92. Usage errors. Change to: She was nearly eighty, but she led an expedition to the Arctic to study the health of the polar bear population to help the government determine whether or not to put polar bear on the endangered species list.
93. Usage error. Change to: As you have told me many times, honesty is the best policy.
94. Usage error. Change to: Finally off her diet, she devoured those fish and chips with her eyes.
95. Usage errors. Change to: As an evangelist, he claimed he led his life based upon sound moral principles.
96. Usage error. Change to: The war is not going well, but the morale of the troops remains high.
97. Subject-verb agreement error. Change to: Neither the Prime Minister nor the Chancellor of the Exchequer has been implicated in the scandal.

98. Dangling modifier. Change to: The pit bull bit yet another child, so the police officer had no choice but to shoot the pit bull dead.
99. Subject-verb agreement error. Change to: Her aquiline nose is one of her features that is particularly striking.
100. Run-on sentence. Change to: He made arrangements to rent a small Volkswagen because he thought it would be the least expensive. He was shocked when he learned how much it costs to rent even a modest car.

Glossary

Adverb: a word which qualifies or modifies a verb (walked <u>quickly</u>) or an adjective (<u>very</u> quick walker) or another adverb (walked <u>very</u> quickly).

Adjective: a word that modifies or qualifies a noun (a <u>beautiful</u> girl) or a pronoun (she is <u>beautiful</u>).

Action verb: see verb.

Active voice: as opposed to passive voice (q.v.), form of verb which depicts subject actively engaged: e.g. 'The baby ate the cookie' as opposed to the less concise passive 'The cookie was eaten by the baby'.

Antecedent: noun to which pronoun refers. In this sentence 'John' is the antecedent for 'him', and 'Mary' is the antecedent for 'she': John saw Mary, but she did not see him.

Auxiliary verb: one which accompanies an action verb to specify the action verb's temporal relationships within the sentence. (She <u>has</u> played football all her life and <u>will</u> play until she <u>can</u> walk no longer.)

Clause: a group of words which contains a subject and a verb; see main clause, independent clause; subordinate clause, dependent clause.

Collective noun: one that describes a group: e.g. team, press, committee.

Comma fault or splice: two sentences incorrectly separated only by a comma.

Complement: see subject complement.

Complex sentence: group of words combining independent and dependent clauses. I am happy, but Jim is not, because the Hotspurs lost.

Compound sentence: group of words containing two independent clauses joined together. I am happy, but Jim is not.

Conjunction: word that joins clauses together.

Coordinate conjunction: short word—and, but, or—that joins words, phrases, or clauses together.

Copula verb: a verb which links together its subject and its subject complement (q.v.), as distinct from an action verb which receives a direct object. (My brother is tall; he was a goalkeeper.) The verb 'to be' (is, am are, was, were, been) is, by far, the most common copula verb.

Dangling modifier: a word, phrase, or clause, usually at the beginning of the sentence and followed by a word it appears to qualify but logically cannot: Looking out of the window, a ragged garden could be seen.

Dependent clause: a group of words which contains a subject and a verb but which cannot stand alone as a sentence.

Direct object: noun or pronoun that follows a verb and identifies who or what. I saw John. John is a teacher.

Faulty parallelism: see parallelism.

Faulty predication: sentence structure error caused by mismatch of subject with verb and its following words. Social scientists study the effects of violence on television influencing children to be violent.

Fused sentence: form of a run-on sentence (q.v.), lacking even the comma between the independent clauses.

Gender-neutral pronouns: those—unlike the gender specific pronouns he, she, him, her—that do not signal gender: it, they, them.

Gerund: a word that is derived from a verb, ends in 'ing', and acts as a noun. Swimming is good exercise.

Imperative mood: command form or mode of a verb, in a sentence typically ending in an exclamation point: Get away from me!

Indefinite pronoun: one that does not specify a specific person: everyone, anybody, all, neither, someone.

Indicative mood: normal mode (i.e. 'mood') of verb, as distinct from subjunctive or imperative moods (q.v.).

Independent clause: a group of words that contains a subject and a verb; a group of words that can stand alone as a sentence; a synonym for a sentence.

Indirect object: noun or pronoun coming between noun and direct object. I will make you a sandwich.

Infinitive: base form of the verb, as preceded by 'to.' To run, to sing, to rest.

Irregular verb: one that does not form its past and past participle (q.v.) by adding 'ed' to its infinitive form (q.v.). (Sing, sang, sung; think, thought.)

Jargon: words and phrases common to certain professions or activities but uncommon to those unfamiliar with those professions or activities: Dr. Smith says he has aortic coarctation.

Lack of agreement in gender: use of one gender-specific pronoun when both are needed: A Member of Parliament must communicate with his [or her] constituents.

Lack of agreement in number: A verb out of sync with its subject—My daughter play tennis—or a pronoun out of sync with its antecedent (q.v.)—A good manager understands the needs of their [his or her] customers.

Main clause: see Independent clause.

Misplaced modifier: a word, phrase, or clause qualifying the wrong word: We ate pancakes with the other guests on paper plates.

Mood: as a verb property, mood identifies mode or manner—indicative, subjunctive, or imperative (q.v.)—in which verb is presented.

Non-restrictive element: word, phrase, or clause not essential to sentence logic, hence separated from rest of sentence by a comma or commas. Among all the candidates, Hardy was the most articulate. See restrictive element.

Noun: a word which identifies a person, a place, a thing, or a state of being; usually serves in a sentence as a subject or object.

Object: a noun or pronoun that receives the action of a verb (he plays piano; he plays it well).

Objective case: Form of pronoun used as object of verb— I know him or preposition Send it to him.

Parallelism: in sentence structure, refers to syntactically equal sentence parts expressed in syntactically equal phrases or clauses; e.g. We are hoping they will arrive on time, praying they will accept the offer, and leaving on Monday.

Participle: see past participle; present participle.

Past participle: verb form used with an auxiliary verb (q.v.).

Passive voice: as opposed to active voice (q.v.), form of verb needed to depict an active object as opposed to an active subject: 'The cookie was eaten by the baby' as opposed to the more concise active 'The baby ate the cookie'.

Possessive case: form of pronoun that indicates ownership— my, not his, her, your book.

Perfect tense: verb form using part of verb 'to have' as auxiliary—I have seen a white robin.

Phrase: group of related words—without a subject and verb— in a sentence.

Preposition, prepositional phrase: a word that links together a noun or pronoun (the object of the preposition) with another part of the sentence, a verb (came for dinner) or a noun (dinner in Paris) to form a phrase.

Present participle: a word derived from a verb, ending in 'ing', and acting as an adjective. A swimming pool.

Pronoun: a word that takes the place of a noun.

Pronoun case: see subjective case, objective case, possessive case.

Reflexive pronoun: one that ends in 'self' and refers back to another pronoun. I can't do it by myself.

Regular verb: as distinct from an irregular verb (q.v.), one which forms its past tense and past participle (q.v.) by adding 'ed' to its infinitive (q.v.) form. (Walk, walked; pick, picked).

Relative pronoun: word such as who, whom, whose, that, which that introduce noun or adjective clauses.

Restrictive element: word, phrase, or clause essential to sentence logic, hence not separated from rest of sentence by comma or commas—A candidate who opposes the war will be elected. See Non-restrictive element.

Run-on Sentence: two complete sentences with insufficient punctuation (usually only a comma) between them. I wanted to watch the French Open, my wife wanted to watch *Extras*.

Sentence fragment: a group of words that is punctuated like a sentence but is less than a sentence. She loves bangers and mash. Which I refuse to eat.

Sexist language: words that should include but ignore one gender, usually the female: policemen are on their way; a police officer must not lose his revolver.

Simple sentence: group of words containing a single main or independent clause. Birds sing.

Split infinitive: base or 'to' form of the verb (e.g. to find) containing a word or phrase between its two parts: to finally find...

Subject complement: a noun or pronoun or adjective which follows a copula verb (q.v.) and identifies or qualifies or modifies the subject of that copula verb: She is a pianist; she is talented.

Subjective case: form of preposition that acts as a subject. He, she, remembers.

Subjunctive mood: verb mode that typically expresses condition contrary to fact—If I were a rich man—or a demand in a 'that' clause—I had to insist that he speak to a manager.

Subordinate clause: see Dependent clause.

Subordinate conjunction: word such as when, although, if, that introduces an adverb clause.

Tense: with mood and voice, one of the properties of a verb that specifies the time of its action, sometimes in the context of other actions.

Verb: a word which usually specifies the action within a clause (q.v.).

Voice: with tense and mood, a property of the verb that specifies the verb's relationship to subject and object. See active voice, passive voice.

Index